Memoirs of Casanova Volume II

Memoirs of Casanova Volume II

Giacomo Casanova

MINT EDITIONS

Memoirs of Casanova Volume II was first published in 1902.

This edition published by Mint Editions 2021.

ISBN 9781513281841 | E-ISBN 9781513286860

Published by Mint Editions®

 MINT
EDITIONS

minteditionbooks.com

Publishing Director: Jennifer Newens
Design & Production: Rachel Lopez Metzger
Project Manager: Micaela Clark
Translated By: Arthur Machen
Typesetting: Westchester Publishing Services

Contents

I

My Misfortunes in Chiozza—Father Stephano—The Lazzaretto at Ancona—The Greek Slave—My Pilgrimage to Our Lady of Loretto—I Go to Rome on Foot, and From Rome to Naples to Meet the Bishop—I Cannot Join Him—Good Luck Offers Me the Means of Reaching Martorano, Which Place I Very Quickly Leave to Return to Naples

The retinue of the ambassador, which was styled "grand," appeared to me very small. It was composed of a Milanese steward, named Carcinelli, of a priest who fulfilled the duties of secretary because he could not write, of an old woman acting as housekeeper, of a man cook with his ugly wife, and eight or ten servants.

We reached Chiozza about noon. Immediately after landing, I politely asked the steward where I should put up, and his answer was:

"Wherever you please, provided you let this man know where it is, so that he can give you notice when the peotta is ready to sail. My duty," he added, "is to leave you at the lazzaretto of Ancona free of expense from the moment we leave this place. Until then enjoy yourself as well as you can."

The man to whom I was to give my address was the captain of the peotta. I asked him to recommend me a lodging.

"You can come to my house," he said, "if you have no objection to share a large bed with the cook, whose wife remains on board."

Unable to devise any better plan, I accepted the offer, and a sailor, carrying my trunk, accompanied me to the dwelling of the honest captain. My trunk had to be placed under the bed which filled up the room. I was amused at this, for I was not in a position to be over-fastidious, and, after partaking of some dinner at the inn, I went about the town. Chiozza is a peninsula, a sea-port belonging to Venice, with a population of ten thousand inhabitants, seamen, fishermen, merchants, lawyers, and government clerks.

I entered a coffee-room, and I had scarcely taken a seat when a young doctor-at-law, with whom I had studied in Padua, came up to me, and introduced me to a druggist whose shop was near by, saying that his house was the rendezvous of all the literary men of the place. A few minutes afterwards, a tall Jacobin friar, blind of one eye, called Corsini, whom I had known in Venice, came in and paid me many compliments. He told me that I had arrived just in time to go to a picnic got up by the Macaronic academicians for the next day, after a sitting of the academy in which every member was to recite something of his composition. He invited me to join them, and to gratify the meeting with the delivery of one of my productions. I accepted the invitation, and, after the reading of ten stanzas which I had written for the occasion, I was unanimously elected a member. My success at the picnic was still greater, for I disposed of such a quantity of macaroni that I was found worthy of the title of prince of the academy.

The young doctor, himself one of the academicians, introduced me to his family. His parents, who were in easy circumstances, received me very kindly. One of his sisters was very amiable, but the other, a professed nun, appeared to me a prodigy of beauty. I might have enjoyed myself in a very agreeable way in the midst of that charming family during my stay in Chiozza, but I suppose that it was my destiny to meet in that place with nothing but sorrows. The young doctor forewarned me that the monk Corsini was a very worthless fellow, despised by everybody, and advised me to avoid him. I thanked him for the information, but my thoughtlessness prevented me from profiting by it. Of a very easy disposition, and too giddy to fear any snares, I was foolish enough to believe that the monk would, on the contrary, be the very man to throw plenty of amusement in my way.

On the third day the worthless dog took me to a house of ill-fame, where I might have gone without his introduction, and, in order to shew my mettle, I obliged a low creature whose ugliness ought to have been a sufficient antidote against any fleshly desire. On leaving the place, he brought me for supper to an inn where we met four scoundrels of his own stamp. After supper one of them began a bank of faro, and I was invited to join in the game. I gave way to that feeling of false pride which so often causes the ruin of young men, and after losing four sequins I expressed a wish to retire, but my honest friend, the Jacobin contrived to make me risk four more sequins in partnership with him. He held the bank, and it was broken. I did not wish to play any more, but Corsini, feigning to pity me and to feel great sorrow at being the cause of my loss, induced me to try myself a bank of twenty-five sequins; my bank was likewise broken. The hope of winning back my money made me keep up the game, and I lost everything I had.

GIACOMO CASANOVA

Deeply grieved, I went away and laid myself down near the cook, who woke up and said I was a libertine.

"You are right," was all I could answer.

I was worn out with fatigue and sorrow, and I slept soundly. My vile tormentor, the monk, woke me at noon, and informed me with a triumphant joy that a very rich young man had been invited by his friends to supper, that he would be sure to play and to lose, and that it would be a good opportunity for me to retrieve my losses.

"I have lost all my money. Lend me twenty sequins."

"When I lend money I am sure to lose; you may call it superstition, but I have tried it too often. Try to find money somewhere else, and come. Farewell."

I felt ashamed to confess my position to my friend, and sending for, a money-lender I emptied my trunk before him. We made an inventory of my clothes, and the honest broker gave me thirty sequins, with the understanding that if I did not redeem them within three days all my things would become his property. I am bound to call him an honest man, for he advised me to keep three shirts, a few pairs of stockings, and a few handkerchiefs; I was disposed to let him take everything, having a presentiment that I would win back all I had lost; a very common error. A few years later I took my revenge by writing a diatribe against presentiments. I am of opinion that the only foreboding in which man can have any sort of faith is the one which forbodes evil, because it comes from the mind, while a presentiment of happiness has its origin in the heart, and the heart is a fool worthy of reckoning foolishly upon fickle fortune.

I did not lose any time in joining the honest company, which was alarmed at the thought of not seeing me. Supper went off without any allusion to gambling, but my admirable qualities were highly praised, and it was decided that a brilliant fortune awaited me in Rome. After supper there was no talk of play, but giving way to my evil genius I loudly asked for my revenge. I was told that if I would take the bank everyone would punt. I took the bank, lost every sequin I had, and retired, begging the monk to pay what I owed to the landlord, which he promised to do.

I was in despair, and to crown my misery I found out as I was going home that I had met the day before with another living specimen of the Greek woman, less beautiful but as perfidious. I went to bed stunned by my grief, and I believe that I must have fainted into a heavy sleep, which lasted eleven hours; my awaking was that of a miserable being, hating the light of heaven, of which he felt himself unworthy, and I closed my eyes again, trying to sleep for a little while longer. I dreaded to rouse myself up entirely, knowing that I would then have to take some decision; but I never once thought of returning to Venice, which would have been the very best thing to do, and I would have destroyed myself rather than confide my sad position to the young doctor. I was weary of my existence, and I entertained vaguely some hope of starving where I was, without leaving my bed. It is certain that I should not have got up if M. Alban, the master of the peotta, had not roused me by calling upon me and informing me that the boat was ready to sail.

The man who is delivered from great perplexity, no matter by what means, feels himself relieved. It seemed to me that Captain Alban had come to point out the only thing I could possibly do; I dressed myself in haste, and tying all my worldly possessions in a handkerchief I went on board. Soon afterwards we left the shore, and in the morning we cast anchor in Orsara, a seaport of Istria. We all landed to visit the city, which would more properly be called a village. It belongs to the Pope, the Republic of Venice having abandoned it to the Holy See.

A young monk of the order of the Recollects who called himself Friar Stephano of Belun, and had obtained a free passage from the devout Captain Alban, joined me as we landed and enquired whether I felt sick.

"Reverend father, I am unhappy."

"You will forget all your sorrow, if you will come and dine with me at the house of one of our devout friends."

I had not broken my fast for thirty-six hours, and having suffered much from sea-sickness during the night, my stomach was quite empty. My erotic inconvenience made me very uncomfortable, my mind felt deeply the consciousness of my degradation, and I did not possess a groat! I was in such a miserable state that I had no strength to accept or to refuse anything. I was thoroughly torpid, and I followed the monk mechanically.

He presented me to a lady, saying that he was accompanying me to Rome, where I intend to become a Franciscan. This untruth disgusted me, and under any other circumstances I would not have let it pass without protest, but in my actual position it struck me as rather comical. The good lady gave us a good dinner of fish cooked in oil, which in Orsara is delicious, and we drank some exquisite refosco. During our meal, a priest happened to drop in, and, after a short conversation, he

GIACOMO CASANOVA

told me that I ought not to pass the night on board the tartan, and pressed me to accept a bed in his house and a good dinner for the next day in case the wind should not allow us to sail; I accepted without hesitation. I offered my most sincere thanks to the good old lady, and the priest took me all over the town. In the evening, he brought me to his house where we partook of an excellent supper prepared by his housekeeper, who sat down to the table with us, and with whom I was much pleased. The refosco, still better than that which I had drunk at dinner, scattered all my misery to the wind, and I conversed gaily with the priest. He offered to read to me a poem of his own composition, but, feeling that my eyes would not keep open, I begged he would excuse me and postpone the reading until the following day.

I went to bed, and in the morning, after ten hours of the most profound sleep, the housekeeper, who had been watching for my awakening, brought me some coffee. I thought her a charming woman, but, alas! I was not in a fit state to prove to her the high estimation in which I held her beauty.

Entertaining feelings of gratitude for my kind host, and disposed to listen attentively to his poem, I dismissed all sadness, and I paid his poetry such compliments that he was delighted, and, finding me much more talented than he had judged me to be at first, he insisted upon treating me to a reading of his idylls, and I had to swallow them, bearing the infliction cheerfully. The day passed off very agreeably; the housekeeper surrounded me with the kindest attentions—a proof that she was smitten with me; and, giving way to that pleasing idea, I felt that, by a very natural system of reciprocity, she had made my conquest. The good priest thought that the day had passed like lightning, thanks to all the beauties I had discovered in his poetry, which, to speak the truth, was below mediocrity, but time seemed to me to drag along very slowly, because the friendly glances of the housekeeper made me long for bedtime, in spite of the miserable condition in which I felt myself morally and physically. But such was my nature; I abandoned myself to joy and happiness, when, had I been more reasonable, I ought to have sunk under my grief and sadness.

But the golden time came at last. I found the pretty housekeeper full of compliance, but only up to a certain point, and as she offered some resistance when I shewed myself disposed to pay a full homage to her charms, I quietly gave up the undertaking, very well pleased for both of us that it had not been carried any further, and I sought my couch in peace. But I had not seen the end of the adventure, for the next morning, when she brought my coffee, her pretty, enticing manners allured me to bestow a few loving caresses upon her, and if she did not abandon herself entirely, it was only, as she said, because she was afraid of some surprise. The day passed off very pleasantly with the good priest, and at night, the house-keeper no longer fearing detection, and I having on my side taken every precaution necessary in the state in which I was, we passed two most delicious hours. I left Orsara the next morning.

Friar Stephano amused me all day with his talk, which plainly showed me his ignorance combined with knavery under the veil of simplicity. He made me look at the alms he had received in Orsara— bread, wine, cheese, sausages, preserves, and chocolate; every nook and cranny of his holy garment was full of provisions.

"Have you received money likewise?" I enquired.

"God forbid! In the first place, our glorious order does not permit me to touch money, and, in the second place, were I to be foolish enough to receive any when I am begging, people would think themselves quit of me with one or two sous, whilst they dive me ten times as much in eatables. Believe me Saint-Francis, was a very judicious man."

I bethought myself that what this monk called wealth would be poverty to me. He offered to share with me, and seemed very proud at my consenting to honour him so far.

The tartan touched at the harbour of Pola, called Veruda, and we landed. After a walk up hill of nearly a quarter of an hour, we entered the city, and I devoted a couple of hours to visiting the Roman antiquities, which are numerous, the town having been the metropolis of the empire. Yet I saw no other trace of grand buildings except the ruins of the arena. We returned to Veruda, and went again to sea. On the following day we sighted Ancona, but the wind being against us we were compelled to tack about, and we did not reach the port till the second day. The harbour of Ancona, although considered one of the great works of Trajan, would be very unsafe if it were not for a causeway which has cost a great deal of money, and which makes it some what better. I observed a fact worthy of notice, namely, that, in the Adriatic, the northern coast has many harbours, while the opposite coast can only boast of one or two. It is evident that the sea is retiring by degrees towards the east, and that in three or four more centuries Venice must be joined to the land. We landed at the old lazzaretto, where we received the pleasant information that we would go through a quarantine of twenty-eight days, because Venice had admitted, after a quarantine of three months, the crew of two ships from Messina, where the plague had recently been raging. I requested a room for myself and for Brother Stephano, who thanked me very heartily. I hired from a Jew a bed, a table and a few chairs, promising to pay for the hire at the expiration of our quarantine. The monk would have nothing but straw. If he had guessed that without him I might have starved, he would most likely not have felt so much vanity at sharing my room. A sailor, expecting to find in me a generous customer, came to enquire where my trunk was, and, hearing from me that I did not know, he, as well as Captain Alban, went to a great deal of trouble to find it, and I could hardly keep down my merriment when the captain called, begging to be excused for having left it behind, and assuring me that he would take care to forward it to me in less than three weeks.

The friar, who had to remain with me four weeks, expected to live at my expense, while, on the contrary, he had been sent by Providence to keep me. He had provisions enough for one week, but it was necessary to think of the future.

After supper, I drew a most affecting picture of my position, shewing that I should be in need of everything until my arrival at Rome, where I was going, I said, to fill the post of secretary of memorials, and my astonishment may be imagined when I saw the blockhead delighted at the recital of my misfortunes.

"I undertake to take care of you until we reach Rome; only tell me whether you can write."

"What a question! Are you joking?"

"Why should I? Look at me; I cannot write anything but my name. True, I can write it with either hand; and what else do I want to know?"

"You astonish me greatly, for I thought you were a priest."

"I am a monk; I say the mass, and, as a matter of course, I must know how to read. Saint-Francis, whose unworthy son I am, could not read, an that is the reason why he never said a mass. But as you can write, you will to-morrow pen a letter in my name to the persons whose names I will give you, and I warrant you we shall have enough sent here to live like fighting cocks all through our quarantine."

The next day he made me write eight letters, because, in the oral tradition of his order, it is said that, when a monk has knocked at seven doors and has met with a refusal at every one of them, he must apply to the eighth with perfect confidence, because there he is certain of receiving alms. As he had already performed the pilgrimage to Rome, he knew every person in Ancona devoted to the cult of Saint-Francis, and was acquainted with the superiors of all the rich convents. I had to write to every person he named, and to set down all the lies he dictated to me. He likewise made me sign the letters for him, saying, that, if he signed himself, his correspondents would see that the letters had not been written by him, which would injure him, for, he added, in this age of corruption, people will esteem only learned men. He compelled me to fill the letters with Latin passages and quotations, even those addressed to ladies, and I remonstrated in vain, for, when I raised any objection, he threatened to leave me without anything to eat. I made up my mind to do exactly as he wished. He desired me to write to the superior of the Jesuits that he would not apply to the Capuchins, because they were no better than atheists, and that that was the reason of the great dislike of Saint-Francis for them. It was in vain that I reminded him of the fact that, in the time of Saint-Francis, there were neither Capuchins nor Recollets. His answer was that I had proved myself an ignoramus. I firmly believed that he would be thought a madman, and that we should not receive anything, but I was mistaken, for such a quantity of provisions came pouring in that I was amazed. Wine was sent from three or four different quarters, more than enough for us during all our stay, and yet I drank nothing but water, so great was my wish to recover my health. As for eatables, enough was sent in every day for six persons; we gave all our surplus to our keeper, who had a large family. But the monk felt no gratitude for the kind souls who bestowed their charity upon him; all his thanks were reserved for Saint-Francis.

He undertook to have my men washed by the keeper; I would not have dared to give it myself, and he said that he had nothing to fear, as everybody was well aware that the monks of his order never wear any kind of linen.

I kept myself in bed nearly all day, and thus avoided shewing myself to visitors. The persons who did not come wrote letters full of incongruities cleverly worded, which I took good care not to point out to him. It was with great difficulty that I tried to persuade him that those letters did not require any answer.

A fortnight of repose and severe diet brought me round towards complete recovery, and I began to walk in the yard of the lazzaretto from morning till night; but the arrival of a Turk from Thessalonia with his family compelled me to suspend my walks, the ground-floor having been given to him. The only pleasure left me was to spend my time on the balcony overlooking the yard. I soon saw a Greek slave, a girl of dazzling beauty, for whom I felt the deepest interest. She was in the habit of spending the whole day sitting near the door with a book or some embroidery in her hand. If she happened to raise her eyes and to meet mine, she modestly bent her head down, and sometimes she rose and went in slowly, as if she meant to say, "I did not know that somebody was looking at me." Her figure was tall and slender, her features proclaimed her to be very young; she had a very fair complexion, with beautiful black hair and eyes. She wore the Greek costume, which gave her person a certain air of very exciting voluptuousness.

I was perfectly idle, and with the temperament which nature and habit had given me, was it likely that I could feast my eyes constantly upon such a charming object without falling desperately in love? I had heard her conversing in Lingua Franca with her master, a fine old man, who, like her, felt very weary of the quarantine, and used to come out but seldom, smoking his pipe, and remaining in the yard only a short time. I felt a great temptation to address a few words to the beautiful girl, but I was afraid she might run away and never come out again; however, unable to control myself any longer, I determined to write to her; I had no difficulty in conveying the letter, as I had only to let it fall from my balcony. But she might have refused to pick it up, and this is the plan I adopted in order not to risk any unpleasant result.

Availing myself of a moment during which she was alone in the yard, I dropped from my balcony a small piece of paper folded like a letter, but I had taken care not to write anything on it, and held the true letter in my hand. As soon as I saw her stooping down to pick up the first, I quickly let the second drop at her feet, and she put both into her pocket. A few minutes afterwards she left the yard. My letter was somewhat to this effect:

"Beautiful angel from the East, I worship you. I will remain all night on this balcony in the hope that you will come to me for a quarter of an hour, and listen to my voice through the hole under my feet. We can speak softly, and in order to hear me you can climb up to the top of the bale of goods which lies beneath the same hole."

I begged from my keeper not to lock me in as he did every night, and he consented on condition that he would watch me, for if I had jumped down in the yard his life might have been the penalty, and he promised not to disturb me on the balcony.

At midnight, as I was beginning to give her up, she came forward. I then laid myself flat on the floor of the balcony, and I placed my head against the hole, about six inches square. I saw her jump on the bale, and her head reached within a foot from the balcony. She was compelled to steady herself with one hand against the wall for fear of falling, and in that position we talked of love, of ardent desires, of obstacles, of impossibilities, and of cunning artifices. I told her the reason for which I dared not jump down in the yard, and she observed that, even without that reason, it would bring ruin upon us, as it would be impossible to come up again, and that, besides, God alone knew what her master would do if he were to find us together. Then, promising to visit me in this way every night, she passed her hand through the hole. Alas! I could not leave off kissing it, for I thought that I had never in my life touched so soft, so delicate a hand. But what bliss when she begged for mine! I quickly thrust my arm through the hole, so that she could fasten her lips to the bend of the elbow. How many sweet liberties my hand ventured to take! But we were at last compelled by prudence to separate, and when I returned to my room I saw with great pleasure that the keeper was fast asleep.

Although I was delighted at having obtained every favour I could possibly wish for in the uncomfortable position we had been in, I racked my brain to contrive the means of securing more complete enjoyment for the following night, but I found during the afternoon that the feminine cunning of my beautiful Greek was more fertile than mine.

Being alone in the yard with her master, she said a few words to him in Turkish, to which he seemed to give his approval, and soon after a servant, assisted by the keeper, brought under the balcony a large basket of goods. She overlooked the arrangement, and in order to secure the basket better, she made the servant place a bale of cotton across two others. Guessing at her purpose, I fairly leaped for joy, for she had found the way of raising herself two feet higher; but I thought that she would then find herself in the most inconvenient position, and that, forced to bend double, she would not be able to resist the fatigue. The hole was not wide enough for her head to pass through, otherwise she might have stood erect and been comfortable. It was necessary at all events to guard against that difficulty; the only way was to tear out one of the planks of the floor of the balcony, but it was not an easy undertaking.

GIACOMO CASANOVA

Yet I decided upon attempting it, regardless of consequences; and I went to my room to provide myself with a large pair of pincers. Luckily the keeper was absent, and availing myself of the opportunity, I succeeded in dragging out carefully the four large nails which fastened the plank. Finding that I could lift it at my will, I replaced the pincers, and waited for the night with amorous impatience.

The darling girl came exactly at midnight, noticing the difficulty she experienced in climbing up, and in getting a footing upon the third bale of cotton, I lifted the plank, and, extending my arm as far as I could, I offered her a steady point of support. She stood straight, and found herself agreeably surprised, for she could pass her head and her arms through the hole. We wasted no time in empty compliments; we only congratulated each other upon having both worked for the same purpose.

If, the night before, I had found myself master of her person more than she was of mine, this time the position was entirely reversed. Her hand roamed freely over every part of my body, but I had to stop half-way down hers. She cursed the man who had packed the bale for not having made it half a foot bigger, so as to get nearer to me. Very likely even that would not have satisfied us, but she would have felt happier.

Our pleasures were barren, yet we kept up our enjoyment until the first streak of light. I put back the plank carefully, and I lay down in my bed in great need of recruiting my strength.

My dear mistress had informed me that the Turkish Bairam began that very morning, and would last three days during which it would be impossible for her to see me.

The night after Bairam, she did not fail to make her appearance, and, saying that she could not be happy without me, she told me that, as she was a Christian woman, I could buy her, if I waited for her after leaving the lazzaretto. I was compelled to tell her that I did not possess the means of doing so, and my confession made her sigh. On the following night, she informed me that her master would sell her for two thousand piasters, that she would give me the amount, that she was yet a virgin, and that I would be pleased with my bargain. She added that she would give me a casket full of diamonds, one of which was alone worth two thousand piasters, and that the sale of the others would place us beyond the reach of poverty for the remainder of our life. She assured me that her master would not notice the loss of the casket, and that, if he did, he would never think of accusing her.

I was in love with this girl; and her proposal made me uncomfortable, but when I woke in the morning I did not hesitate any longer. She brought the casket in the evening, but I told her that I never could make up my mind to be accessory to a robbery; she was very unhappy, and said that my love was not as deep as her own, but that she could not help admiring me for being so good a Christian.

This was the last night; probably we should never meet again. The flame of passion consumed us. She proposed that I should lift her up to the balcony through the open space. Where is the lover who would have objected to so attractive a proposal? I rose, and without being a Milo, I placed my hands under her arms, I drew her up towards me, and my desires are on the point of being fulfilled. Suddenly I feel two hands upon my shoulders, and the voice of the keeper exclaims, "What are you about?" I let my precious burden drop; she regains her chamber, and I, giving vent to my rage, throw myself flat on the floor of the balcony, and remain there without a movement, in spite of the shaking of the keeper whom I was sorely tempted to strangle. At last I rose from the floor and went to bed without uttering one word, and not even caring to replace the plank.

In the morning, the governor informed us that we were free. As I left the lazzaretto, with a breaking heart, I caught a glimpse of the Greek slave drowned in tears.

I agreed to meet Friar Stephano at the exchange, and I took the Jew from whom I had hired the furniture, to the convent of the Minims, where I received from Father Lazari ten sequins and the address of the bishop, who, after performing quarantine on the frontiers of Tuscany, had proceeded to Rome, where he would expect me to meet him.

I paid the Jew, and made a poor dinner at an inn. As I was leaving it to join the monk, I was so unlucky as to meet Captain Alban, who reproached me bitterly for having led him to believe that my trunk had been left behind. I contrived to appease his anger by telling him all my misfortunes, and I signed a paper in which I declared that I had no claim whatever upon him. I then purchased a pair of shoes and an overcoat, and met Stephano, whom I informed of my decision to make a pilgrimage to Our Lady of Loretto. I said I would await there for him, and that we would afterwards travel together as far as Rome. He answered that he did not wish to go through Loretto, and that I would repent of my contempt for the grace of Saint-Francis. I did not alter my mind, and I left for Loretto the next day in the enjoyment of perfect health.

GIACOMO CASANOVA

I reached the Holy City, tired almost to death, for it was the first time in my life that I had walked fifteen miles, drinking nothing but water, although the weather was very warm, because the dry wine used in that part of the country parched me too much. I must observe that, in spite of my poverty, I did not look like a beggar.

As I was entering the city, I saw coming towards me an elderly priest of very respectable appearance, and, as he was evidently taking notice of me, as soon as he drew near, I saluted him, and enquired where I could find a comfortable inn. "I cannot doubt," he said, "that a person like you, travelling on foot, must come here from devout motives; come with me." He turned back, I followed him, and he took me to a fine-looking house. After whispering a few words to a man who appeared to be a steward, he left me saying, very affably, "You shall be well attended to."

My first impression was that I had been mistaken for some other person, but I said nothing.

I was led to a suite of three rooms; the chamber was decorated with damask hangings, the bedstead had a canopy, and the table was supplied with all materials necessary for writing. A servant brought me a light dressing-gown, and another came in with linen and a large tub full of water, which he placed before me; my shoes and stockings were taken off, and my feet washed. A very decent-looking woman, followed by a servant girl, came in a few minutes after, and curtsying very low, she proceeded to make my bed. At that moment the Angelus bell was heard; everyone knelt down, and I followed their example. After the prayer, a small table was neatly laid out, I was asked what sort of wine I wished to drink, and I was provided with newspapers and two silver candlesticks. An hour afterwards I had a delicious fish supper, and, before I retired to bed, a servant came to enquire whether I would take chocolate in the morning before or after mass.

As soon as I was in bed, the servant brought me a night-lamp with a dial, and I remained alone. Except in France I have never had such a good bed as I had that night. It would have cured the most chronic insomnia, but I was not labouring under such a disease, and I slept for ten hours.

This sort of treatment easily led me to believe that I was not in any kind of hostelry; but where was I? How was I to suppose that I was in a hospital?

When I had taken my chocolate, a hair-dresser—quite a fashionable, dapper fellow—made his appearance, dying to give vent to his chattering propensities. Guessing that I did not wish to be shaved, he offered to clip my soft down with the scissors, saying that I would look younger.

"Why do you suppose that I want to conceal my age?"

"It is very natural, because, if your lordship did not wish to do so, your lordship would have shaved long ago. Countess Marcolini is here; does your lordship know her? I must go to her at noon to dress her hair."

I did not feel interested in the Countess Marcolini, and, seeing it, the gossip changed the subject.

"Is this your lordship's first visit to this house? It is the finest hospital throughout the papal states."

"I quite agree with you, and I shall compliment His Holiness on the establishment."

"Oh! His Holiness knows all about it, he resided here before he became pope. If Monsignor Caraffa had not been well acquainted with you, he would not have introduced you here."

Such is the use of barbers throughout Europe; but you must not put any questions to them, for, if you do, they are sure to threat you to an impudent mixture of truth and falsehood, and instead of you pumping them, they will worm everything out of you.

Thinking that it was my duty to present my respectful compliments to Monsignor Caraffa, I desired to be taken to his apartment. He gave me a pleasant welcome, shewed me his library, and entrusted me to the care of one of his abbes, a man of parts, who acted as my cicerone every where. Twenty years afterwards, this same abbe was of great service to me in Rome, and, if still alive, he is a canon of St. John Lateran.

On the following day, I took the communion in the Santa-Casa. The third day was entirely employed in examining the exterior of this truly wonderful sanctuary, and early the next day I resumed my journey, having spent nothing except three paoli for the barber. Halfway to Macerata, I overtook Brother Stephano walking on at a very slow rate. He was delighted to see me again, and told me that he had left Ancona two hours after me, but that he never walked more than three miles a day, being quite satisfied to take two months for a journey which, even on foot, can easily be accomplished in a week. "I want," he said, "to reach Rome without fatigue and in good health. I am in no hurry, and if you feel disposed to travel with me and in the same quiet way, Saint-Francis will not find it difficult to keep us both during the journey."

This lazy fellow was a man about thirty, red-haired, very strong and healthy; a true peasant who had turned himself into a monk only for the sake of living in idle comfort. I answered that, as I was in a hurry to reach Rome, I could not be his travelling companion.

"I undertake to walk six miles, instead of three, today," he said, "if you will carry my cloak, which I find very heavy."

The proposal struck me as a rather funny one; I put on his cloak, and he took my great-coat, but, after the exchange, we cut such a comical figure that every peasant we met laughed at us. His cloak would truly have proved a load for a mule. There were twelve pockets quite full, without taken into account a pocket behind, which he called 'il batticulo', and which contained alone twice as much as all the others. Bread, wine, fresh and salt meat, fowls, eggs, cheese, ham, sausages— everything was to be found in those pockets, which contained provisions enough for a fortnight.

I told him how well I had been treated in Loretto, and he assured me that I might have asked Monsignor Caraffa to give me letters for all the hospitals on my road to Rome, and that everywhere I would have met with the same reception. "The hospitals," he added, "are all under the curse of Saint-Francis, because the mendicant friars are not admitted in them; but we do not mind their gates being shut against us, because they are too far apart from each other. We prefer the homes of the persons attached to our order; these we find everywhere."

"Why do you not ask hospitality in the convents of your order?"

"I am not so foolish. In the first place, I should not be admitted, because, being a fugitive, I have not the written obedience which must be shown at every convent, and I should even run the risk of being thrown into prison; your monks are a cursed bad lot. In the second place, I should not be half so comfortable in the convents as I am with our devout benefactors."

"Why and how are you a fugitive?"

He answered my question by the narrative of his imprisonment and flight, the whole story being a tissue of absurdities and lies. The fugitive Recollet friar was a fool, with something of the wit of harlequin, and he thought that every man listening to him was a greater fool than himself. Yet with all his folly he was not went in a certain species of cunning. His religious principles were singular. As he did not wish to be taken for a bigoted man he was scandalous, and for the sake of making people laugh he would often make use of the most disgusting expressions. He had no taste whatever for women, and no inclination towards the pleasures of the flesh; but this was only owing to a deficiency in his natural temperament, and yet he claimed for himself the virtue of continence. On that score, everything appeared to him food for merriment, and when he had drunk rather too much, he would ask questions of such an indecent character that they would bring blushes on everybody's countenance. Yet the brute would only laugh.

As we were getting within one hundred yards from the house of the devout friend whom he intended to honour with his visit, he took back his heavy cloak. On entering the house he gave his blessing to everybody, and everyone in the family came to kiss his hand. The mistress of the house requested him to say mass for them, and the compliant monk asked to be taken to the vestry, but when I whispered in his ear,—

"Have you forgotten that we have already broken our fast to-day?" he answered, dryly,—

"Mind your own business."

I dared not make any further remark, but during the mass I was indeed surprised, for I saw that he did not understand what he was doing. I could not help being amused at his awkwardness, but I had not yet seen the best part of the comedy. As soon as he had somehow or other finished his mass he went to the confessional, and after hearing in confession every member of the family he took it into his head to refuse absolution to the daughter of his hostess, a girl of twelve or thirteen, pretty and quite charming. He gave his refusal publicly, scolding her and threatening her with the torments of hell. The poor girl, overwhelmed with shame, left the church crying bitterly, and I, feeling real sympathy for her, could not help saying aloud to Stephano that he was a madman. I ran after the girl to offer her my consolations, but she had disappeared, and could not be induced to join us at dinner. This piece of extravagance on the part of the monk exasperated me to such an extent that I felt a very strong inclination to thrash him. In the presence of all the family I told him that he was an impostor, and the infamous destroyer of the poor child's honour; I challenged him to explain his reasons for refusing to give her absolution, but he closed my lips by answering very coolly that he could not betray the secrets of the confessional. I could eat nothing, and was fully determined to leave the scoundrel. As we left the house I was compelled to accept one paolo as the price of the mock mass he had said. I had to fulfil the sorry duty of his treasurer.

The moment we were on the road, I told him that I was going to part company, because I was afraid of being sent as a felon to the galleys if I continued my journey with him. We exchanged high words; I called him an ignorant scoundrel, he styled me beggar. I struck him a violent slap on the face, which he returned with a blow from his stick, but I quickly snatched it from him, and, leaving him, I hastened towards Macerata. A carrier who was going to Tolentino took me with him for two paoli, and for six more I might have reached Foligno in a waggon, but unfortunately a wish for economy made me refuse the offer. I felt well, and I thought I could easily walk as far as Valcimare, but I arrived there only after five hours of hard walking, and thoroughly beaten with fatigue. I was strong and healthy, but a walk of five hours was more than I could bear, because in my infancy I had never gone a league on foot. Young people cannot practise too much the art of walking.

The next day, refreshed by a good night's rest, and ready to resume my journey, I wanted to pay the innkeeper, but, alas! a new misfortune was in store for me! Let the reader imagine my sad position! I recollected that I had forgotten my purse, containing seven sequins, on the table of the inn at Tolentino. What a thunderbolt! I was in despair, but I gave up the idea of going back, as it was very doubtful whether I would find my money. Yet it contained all I possessed, save a few copper coins I had in my pocket. I paid my small bill, and, deeply grieved at my loss, continued my journey towards Seraval. I was within three miles of that place when, in jumping over a ditch, I sprained my ankle, and was compelled to sit down on one side of the road, and to wait until someone should come to my assistance.

In the course of an hour a peasant happened to pass with his donkey, and he agreed to carry me to Seraval for one paolo. As I wanted to spend as little as possible, the peasant took me to an ill-looking fellow who, for two paoli paid in advance, consented to give me a lodging. I asked him to send for a surgeon, but I did not obtain one until the following morning. I had a wretched supper, after which I lay down in a filthy bed. I was in hope that sleep would bring me some relief, but my evil genius was preparing for me a night of torments.

Three men, armed with guns and looking like banditti, came in shortly after I had gone to bed, speaking a kind of slang which I could not make out, swearing, raging, and paying no attention to me. They drank and sang until midnight, after which they threw themselves down on bundles of straw brought for them, and my host, who was drunk, came, greatly to my dismay, to lie down near me. Disgusted at the idea of having such a fellow for my bed companion, I refused to let him come, but he answered, with fearful blasphemies, that all the devils in hell could not prevent him from taking possession of his own bed. I was forced to make room for him, and exclaimed "Heavens, where am I?" He told me that I was in the house of the most honest constable in all the papal states.

Could I possibly have supposed that the peasant would have brought me amongst those accursed enemies of humankind!

He laid himself down near me, but the filthy scoundrel soon compelled me to give him, for certain reasons, such a blow in his chest that he rolled out of bed. He picked himself up, and renewed his beastly attempt. Being well aware that I could not master him without great danger, I got out of bed, thinking myself lucky that he did not oppose my wish, and crawling along as well as I could, I found a chair on which I passed the night. At day-break, my tormentor, called up by his honest comrades, joined them in drinking and shouting, and the three strangers, taking their guns, departed. Left alone by the departure of the vile rabble, I passed another unpleasant hour, calling in vain for someone. At last a young boy came in, I gave him some money and he went for a surgeon. The doctor examined my foot, and assured me that three or four days would set me to rights. He advised me to be removed to an inn, and I most willingly followed his counsel. As soon as I was brought to the inn, I went to bed, and was well cared for, but my position was such that I dreaded the moment of my recovery. I feared that I should be compelled to sell my coat to pay the inn-keeper, and the very thought made me feel ashamed. I began to consider that if I had controlled my sympathy for the young girl so ill-treated by Stephano, I should not have fallen into this sad predicament, and I felt conscious that my sympathy had been a mistake. If I had put up with the faults of the friar, if this and if that, and every other if was conjured up to torment my restless and wretched brain. Yet I must confess that the thoughts which have their origin in misfortune are not without advantage to a young man, for they give him the habit of thinking, and the man who does not think never does anything right.

The morning of the fourth day came, and I was able to walk, as the surgeon had predicted; I made up my mind, although reluctantly, to beg the worthy man to sell my great coat for me—a most unpleasant necessity, for rain had begun to fall. I owed fifteen paoli to the inn-keeper and four to the surgeon. Just as I was going to proffer my painful request, Brother Stephano made his appearance in my room, and burst into loud laughter enquiring whether I had forgotten the blow from his stick!

I was struck with amazement! I begged the surgeon to leave me with the monk, and he immediately complied.

I must ask my readers whether it is possible, in the face of such extraordinary circumstances, not to feel superstitious! What is truly miraculous in this case is the precise minute at which the event took place, for the friar entered the room as the word was hanging on my lips. What surprised me most was the force of Providence, of fortune, of chance, whatever name is given to it, of that very necessary combination which compelled me to find no hope but in that fatal monk, who had begun to be my protective genius in Chiozza at the moment my distress had likewise commenced. And yet, a singular guardian angel, this Stephano! I felt that the mysterious force which threw me in his hands was a punishment rather than a favour.

Nevertheless he was welcome, because I had no doubt of his relieving me from my difficulties,—and whatever might be the power that sent him to me, I felt that I could not do better than to submit to its influence; the destiny of that monk was to escort me to Rome.

"Chi va piano va sano," said the friar as soon as we were alone. He had taken five days to traverse the road over which I had travelled in one day, but he was in good health, and he had met with no misfortune. He told me that, as he was passing, he heard that an abbe, secretary to the Venetian ambassador at Rome, was lying ill at the inn, after having been robbed in Valcimara. "I came to see you," he added, "and as I find you recovered from your illness, we can start again together; I agree to walk six miles every day to please you. Come, let us forget the past, and let us be at once on our way."

"I cannot go; I have lost my purse, and I owe twenty paoli."

"I will go and find the amount in the name of Saint-Francis."

He returned within an hour, but he was accompanied by the infamous constable who told me that, if I had let him know who I was, he would have been happy to keep me in his house. "I will give you," he continued, "forty paoli, if you will promise me the protection of your ambassador; but if you do not succeed in obtaining it for me in Rome, you will undertake to repay me. Therefore you must give me an acknowledgement of the debt."

"I have no objection." Every arrangement was speedily completed; I received the money, paid my debts, and left Seraval with Stephano.

About one o'clock in the afternoon, we saw a wretched-looking house at a short distance from the road, and the friar said, "It is a good distance from here to Collefiorito; we had better put up there for the night." It was in vain that I objected, remonstrating that we were certain of having very poor accommodation! I had to submit to his will. We found a decrepit old man lying on a pallet, two ugly women of thirty or forty, three children entirely naked, a cow, and a cursed dog which barked continually. It was a picture of squalid misery; but the niggardly monk, instead of giving alms to the poor people, asked them to entertain us to supper in the name of Saint-Francis.

"You must boil the hen," said the dying man to the females, "and bring out of the cellar the bottle of wine which I have kept now for twenty years." As he uttered those few words, he was seized with such a fit of coughing that I thought he would die. The friar went near him, and promised him that, by the grace of Saint-Francis, he would get young and well. Moved by the sight of so much misery, I wanted to continue my journey as far as Collefiorito, and to wait there for Stephano, but the women would not let me go, and I remained. After boiling for four hours the hen set the strongest teeth at defiance, and the bottle which I uncorked proved to be nothing but sour vinegar. Losing patience, I got hold of the monk's batticaslo, and took out of it enough for a plentiful supper, and I saw the two women opening their eyes very wide at the sight of our provisions.

We all ate with good appetite, and, after our supper the women made for us two large beds of fresh straw, and we lay down in the dark, as the last bit of candle to be found in the miserable dwelling was burnt out. We had not been lying on the straw five minutes, when Stephano called out to me that one of the women had just placed herself near him, and at the same instant the other one takes me in her arms and kisses me. I push her away, and the monk defends himself against the other; but mine, nothing daunted, insists upon laying herself near me; I get up, the dog springs at my neck, and fear compels me to remain quiet on my straw bed; the monk screams, swears, struggles, the dog barks furiously, the old man coughs; all is noise and confusion. At last Stephano, protected by his heavy garments, shakes off the too loving shrew, and, braving the dog, manages to find his stick. Then he lays about to right and left, striking in every direction; one of the women exclaims, "Oh, God!" the friar answers, "She has her quietus." Calm reigns again in the house, the dog, most likely dead, is silent; the old man, who perhaps has received his death-blow, coughs no more; the children sleep, and the women, afraid of the singular caresses of the monk, sheer off into a corner; the remainder of the night passed off quietly.

At day-break I rose; Stephano was likewise soon up. I looked all round, and my surprise was great when I found that the women had gone out, and seeing that the old man gave no sign of life, and had a bruise on his forehead, I shewed it to Stephano, remarking that very likely he had killed him.

"It is possible," he answered, "but I have not done it intentionally."

Then taking up his batticulo and finding it empty he flew into a violent passion; but I was much pleased, for I had been afraid that the women had gone out to get assistance and to have us arrested, and the robbery of our provisions reassured me, as I felt certain that the poor wretches had gone out of the way so as to secure impunity for their theft. But I laid great stress upon the danger we should run by remaining any longer, and I succeeded in frightening the friar out of the house. We soon met a waggoner going to Folligno; I persuaded Stephano to take the opportunity of putting a good distance between us and the scene of our last adventures; and, as we were eating our breakfast at Folligno, we saw another waggon, quite empty, got a lift in it for a trifle, and thus rode to Pisignano, where a devout person gave us a charitable welcome, and I slept soundly through the night without the dread of being arrested.

Early the next day we reached Spoleti, where Brother Stephano had two benefactors, and, careful not to give either of them a cause of jealousy, he favoured both; we dined with the first, who entertained us like princes, and we had supper and lodging in the house of the second, a wealthy wine merchant, and the father of a large and delightful family. He gave us a delicious supper, and everything would have gone on pleasantly had not the friar, already excited by his good dinner, made himself quite drunk. In that state, thinking to please his new host, he began to abuse the other, greatly to my annoyance; he said the wine he had given us to drink was adulterated, and that the man was a thief. I gave him the lie to his face, and called him a scoundrel. The host and his wife pacified me, saying that they were well acquainted with their neighbour, and knew what to think of him; but the monk threw his napkin at my face, and the host took him very quietly by the arm and put him to bed in a room in which he locked him up. I slept in another room.

In the morning I rose early, and was considering whether it would not be better to go alone, when the friar, who had slept himself sober, made his appearance and told me that we ought for the future to live together like good friends, and not give way to angry feelings; I followed my destiny once more. We resumed our journey, and at Soma, the inn-keeper, a woman of rare beauty, gave us a good dinner, and some excellent Cyprus wine which the Venetian couriers exchanged with her against delicious truffles found in the vicinity of Soma, which sold for a good price in Venice. I did not leave the handsome inn-keeper without losing a part of my heart.

It would be difficult to draw a picture of the indignation which overpowered me when, as we were about two miles from Terni, the infamous friar shewed me a small bag full of truffles which the scoundrel had stolen from the amiable woman by way of thanks for her generous hospitality. The truffles were worth two sequins at least. In my indignation I snatched the bag from him, saying that I would certainly return it to its lawful owner. But, as he had not committed the robbery to give himself the pleasure of making restitution, he threw himself upon me, and we came to a regular fight. But victory did not remain long in abeyance; I forced his stick out of his hands, knocked him into a ditch, and went off. On reaching Terni, I wrote a letter of apology to our beautiful hostess of Soma, and sent back the truffles.

From Terni I went on foot to Otricoli, where I only stayed long enough to examine the fine old bridge, and from there I paid four paoli to a waggoner who carried me to Castel-Nuovo, from which place I walked to Rome. I reached the celebrated city on the 1st of September, at nine in the morning.

I must not forget to mention here a rather peculiar circumstance, which, however ridiculous it may be in reality, will please many of my readers.

An hour after I had left Castel-Nuovo, the atmosphere being calm and the sky clear, I perceived on my right, and within ten paces of me, a pyramidal flame about two feet long and four or five feet above the ground. This apparition surprised me, because it seemed to accompany me. Anxious to examine it, I endeavoured to get nearer to it, but the more I advanced towards it the further it went from me. It would stop when I stood still, and when the road along which I was travelling happened to be lined with trees, I no longer saw it, but it was sure to reappear as soon as I reached a portion of the road without trees. I several times retraced my steps purposely, but, every time I did so, the flame disappeared, and would not shew itself again until I proceeded towards Rome. This extraordinary beacon left me when daylight chased darkness from the sky.

What a splendid field for ignorant superstition, if there had been any witnesses to that phenomenon, and if I had chanced to make a great name in Rome! History is full of such trifles, and the world is full of people who attach great importance to them in spite of the so-called light of science. I must candidly confess that, although somewhat versed in physics, the sight of that small meteor gave me singular ideas. But I was prudent enough not to mention the circumstance to any one.

When I reached the ancient capital of the world, I possessed only seven paoli, and consequently I did not loiter about. I paid no attention to the splendid entrance through the gate of the polar trees, which is by mistake pompously called of the people, or to the beautiful square of the same name, or to the portals of the magnificent churches, or to all the stately buildings which generally strike the traveller as he enters the city. I went straight towards Monte-Magnanopoli, where, according to the address given to me, I was to find the bishop. There I was informed that he had left Rome ten days before, leaving instructions to send me to Naples free of expense. A coach was to start for Naples the next day; not caring to see Rome, I went to bed until the time for the departure of the coach. I travelled with three low fellows to whom I did not address one word through the whole of the journey. I entered Naples on the 6th day of September.

I went immediately to the address which had been given to me in Rome; the bishop was not there. I called at the Convent of the Minims, and I found that he had left Naples to proceed to Martorano. I enquired whether he had left any instructions for me, but all in vain, no one could give me any information. And there I was, alone in a large city, without a friend, with eight carlini in my pocket, and not knowing what to do! But never mind; fate calls me to Martorano, and to Martorano I must go. The distance, after all, is only two hundred miles.

I found several drivers starting for Cosenza, but when they heard that I had no luggage, they refused to take me, unless I paid in advance. They were quite right, but their prudence placed me under the necessity of going on foot. Yet I felt I must reach Martorano, and I made up my mind to walk the distance, begging food and lodging like the very reverend Brother Stephano.

First of all I made a light meal for one fourth of my money, and, having been informed that I had to follow the Salerno road, I went towards Portici where I arrived in an hour and a half. I already felt rather fatigued; my legs, if not my head, took me to an inn, where I ordered a room and some supper. I was served in good style, my appetite was excellent, and I passed a quiet night in a comfortable bed. In the morning I told the inn-keeper that I would return for my dinner, and I went out to visit the royal palace. As I passed through the gate, I was met by a man of prepossessing appearance, dressed in the eastern fashion, who offered to shew me all over the palace, saying that I would thus save my money. I was in a position to accept any offer; I thanked him for his kindness.

Happening during the conversation to state that I was a Venetian, he told me that he was my subject, since he came from Zante. I acknowledged his polite compliment with a reverence.

"I have," he said, "some very excellent muscatel wine 'grown in the East, which I could sell you cheap."

"I might buy some, but I warn you I am a good judge."

"So much the better. Which do you prefer?"

"The Cerigo wine."

"You are right. I have some rare Cerigo muscatel, and we can taste it if you have no objection to dine with me."

"None whatever."

"I can likewise give you the wines of Samos and Cephalonia. I have also a quantity of minerals, plenty of vitriol, cinnabar, antimony, and one hundred quintals of mercury."

"Are all these goods here?"

"No, they are in Naples. Here I have only the muscatel wine and the mercury."

It is quite naturally and without any intention to deceive, that a young man accustomed to poverty, and ashamed of it when he speaks to a rich stranger, boasts of his means—of his fortune. As I was talking with my new acquaintance, I recollected an amalgam of mercury with lead and bismuth, by which the mercury increases one-fourth in weight. I said nothing, but I bethought myself that if the mystery should be unknown to the Greek I might profit by it. I felt that some cunning was necessary, and that he would not care for my secret if I proposed to sell it to him without preparing the way. The best plan was to astonish my man with the miracle of the augmentation of the mercury, treat it as a jest, and see what his intentions would be. Cheating is a crime, but honest cunning may be considered as a species of prudence. True, it is a quality which is near akin to roguery; but that cannot be helped, and the man who, in time of need, does not know how to exercise his cunning nobly is a fool. The Greeks call this sort of wisdom Cerdaleophyon from the word cerdo; fox, and it might be translated by foxdom if there were such a word in English.

After we had visited the palace we returned to the inn, and the Greek took me to his room, in which he ordered the table to be laid for two. In the next room I saw several large vessels of muscatel wine and four flagons of mercury, each containing about ten pounds.

My plans were laid, and I asked him to let me have one of the flagons of mercury at the current price, and took it to my room. The Greek went out to attend to his business, reminding me that he expected me to dinner. I went out likewise, and bought two pounds and a half of lead and an equal quantity of bismuth; the druggist had no more. I came back to the inn, asked for some large empty bottles, and made the amalgam.

We dined very pleasantly, and the Greek was delighted because I pronounced his Cerigo excellent. In the course of conversation he inquired laughingly why I had bought one of his flagons of mercury.

"You can find out if you come to my room," I said.

After dinner we repaired to my room, and he found his mercury divided in two vessels. I asked for a piece of chamois, strained the liquid through it, filled his own flagon, and the Greek stood astonished at the sight of the fine mercury, about one-fourth of a flagon, which remained over, with an equal quantity of a powder unknown to him; it was the bismuth. My merry laugh kept company with his astonishment, and calling one of the servants of the inn I sent him to the druggist to sell the mercury that was left. He returned in a few minutes and handed me fifteen carlini.

The Greek, whose surprise was complete, asked me to give him back his own flagon, which was there quite full, and worth sixty carlini. I handed it to him with a smile, thanking him for the opportunity he had afforded me of earning fifteen carlini, and took care to add that I should leave for Salerno early the next morning.

"Then we must have supper together this evening," he said.

During the afternoon we took a walk towards Mount Vesuvius. Our conversation went from one subject to another, but no allusion was made to the mercury, though I could see that the Greek had something on his mind. At supper he told me, jestingly, that I ought to stop in Portici the next day to make forty-five carlini out of the three other flagons of mercury. I answered gravely that I did not want the money, and that I had augmented the first flagon only for the sake of procuring him an agreeable surprise.

"But," said he, "you must be very wealthy."

"No, I am not, because I am in search of the secret of the augmentation of gold, and it is a very expensive study for us."

"How many are there in your company?"

"Only my uncle and myself."

"What do you want to augment gold for? The augmentation of mercury ought to be enough for you. Pray, tell me whether the mercury augmented by you to-day is again susceptible of a similar increase."

"No, if it were so, it would be an immense source of wealth for us."

"I am much pleased with your sincerity."

Supper over I paid my bill, and asked the landlord to get me a carriage and pair of horses to take me to Salerno early the next morning. I thanked the Greek for his delicious muscatel wine, and, requesting his address in Naples, I assured him that he would see me within a fortnight, as I was determined to secure a cask of his Cerigo.

We embraced each other, and I retired to bed well pleased with my day's work, and in no way astonished at the Greek's not offering to purchase my secret, for I was certain that he would not sleep for anxiety, and that I should see him early in the morning. At all events, I had enough money to reach the Tour-du-Grec, and there Providence would take care of me. Yet it seemed to me very difficult to travel as far as Martorano, begging like a mendicant-friar, because my outward appearance did not excite pity; people would feel interested in me only from a conviction that I needed nothing—a very unfortunate conviction, when the object of it is truly poor.

As I had forseen, the Greek was in my room at daybreak. I received him in a friendly way, saying that we could take coffee together.

"Willingly; but tell me, reverend abbe, whether you would feel disposed to sell me your secret?"

"Why not? When we meet in Naples—"

"But why not now?"

"I am expected in Salerno; besides, I would only sell the secret for a large sum of money, and I am not acquainted with you."

"That does not matter, as I am sufficiently known here to pay you in cash. How much would you want?"

"Two thousand ounces."

"I agree to pay you that sum provided that I succeed in making the augmentation myself with such matter as you name to me, which I will purchase."

"It is impossible, because the necessary ingredients cannot be got here; but they are common enough in Naples."

"If it is any sort of metal, we can get it at the Tourdu-Grec. We could go there together. Can you tell me what is the expense of the augmentation?"

"One and a half per cent. but are you likewise known at the Tour-du-Grec, for I should not like to lose my time?"

"Your doubts grieve me."

Saying which, he took a pen, wrote a few words, and handed to me this order:

"At sight, pay to bearer the sum of fifty gold ounces, on account of Panagiotti."

He told me that the banker resided within two hundred yards of the inn, and he pressed me to go there myself. I did not stand upon ceremony, but went to the banker who paid me the amount. I returned to my room in which he was waiting for me, and placed the gold on the table, saying that we could now proceed together to the Tour-du-Grec, where we would complete our arrangements after the signature of a deed of agreement. The Greek had his own carriage and horses; he gave orders for them to be got ready, and we left the inn; but he had nobly insisted upon my taking possession of the fifty ounces.

When we arrived at the Tour-du-Grec, he signed a document by which he promised to pay me two thousand ounces as soon as I should have discovered to him the process of augmenting mercury by one-fourth without injuring its quality, the amalgam to be equal to the mercury which I had sold in his presence at Portici.

He then gave me a bill of exchange payable at sight in eight days on M. Genaro de Carlo. I told him that the ingredients were lead and bismuth; the first, combining with mercury, and the second giving to the whole the perfect fluidity necessary to strain it through the chamois leather. The Greek went out to try the amalgam—I do not know where, and I dined alone, but toward evening he came back, looking very disconsolate, as I had expected.

"I have made the amalgam," he said, "but the mercury is not perfect."

"It is equal to that which I have sold in Portici, and that is the very letter of your engagement."

"But my engagement says likewise without injury to the quality. You must agree that the quality is injured, because it is no longer susceptible of further augmentation."

"You knew that to be the case; the point is its equality with the mercury I sold in Portici. But we shall have to go to law, and you will lose. I am sorry the secret should become public. Congratulate yourself, sir, for, if you should gain the lawsuit, you will have obtained my secret for nothing. I would never have believed you capable of deceiving me in such a manner."

"Reverend sir, I can assure you that I would not willingly deceive any one."

"Do you know the secret, or do you not? Do you suppose I would have given it to you without the agreement we entered into? Well, there will be some fun over this affair in Naples, and the lawyers will make money out of it. But I am much grieved at this turn of affairs, and I am very sorry that I allowed myself to be so easily deceived by your fine talk. In the mean time, here are your fifty ounces."

As I was taking the money out of my pocket, frightened to death lest he should accept it, he left the room, saying that he would not have it. He soon returned; we had supper in the same room, but at separate tables; war had been openly declared, but I felt certain that a treaty of peace would soon be signed. We did not exchange one word during the evening, but in the morning he came to me as I was getting ready to go. I again offered to return the money I received, but he told me to keep it, and proposed to give me fifty ounces more if I would give him back his bill of exchange for two thousand. We began to argue the matter quietly, and after two hours of discussion I gave in. I received fifty ounces more, we dined together like old friends, and embraced each other cordially. As I was bidding him adieu, he gave me an order on his house at Naples for a barrel of muscatel wine, and he presented me with a splendid box containing twelve razors with silver handles, manufactured in the Tour-du-Grec. We parted the best friends in the world and well pleased with each other.

I remained two days in Salerno to provide myself with linen and other necessaries. Possessing about one hundred sequins, and enjoying good health, I was very proud of my success, in which I could not see any cause of reproach to myself, for the cunning I had brought into play to insure the sale of my secret could not be found fault with except by the most intolerant of moralists, and such men have no authority to speak on matters of business. At all events, free, rich, and certain of presenting myself before the bishop with a respectable appearance, and not like a beggar, I soon recovered my natural spirits, and congratulated myself upon having bought sufficient experience to insure me against falling a second time an easy prey to a Father Corsini, to thieving gamblers, to mercenary women, and particularly to the impudent scoundrels who barefacedly praise so well those they intend to dupe—a species of knaves very common in the world, even amongst people who form what is called good society.

I left Salerno with two priests who were going to Cosenza on business, and we traversed the distance of one hundred and forty-two miles in twenty-two hours. The day after my arrival in the capital of Calabria, I took a small carriage and drove to Martorano. During the journey, fixing my eyes upon the famous mare Ausonaum, I felt delighted at finding myself in the middle of Magna Grecia, rendered so celebrated for twenty-four centuries by its connection with Pythagoras. I looked with astonishment upon a country renowned for its fertility, and in which, in spite of nature's prodigality, my eyes met everywhere the aspect of terrible misery, the complete absence of that pleasant superfluity which helps man to enjoy life, and the degradation of the inhabitants sparsely scattered on a soil where they ought to be so numerous; I felt ashamed to acknowledge them as originating from the same stock as myself. Such is, however the Terra di Lavoro where labour seems to be execrated, where everything is cheap, where the miserable inhabitants consider that they have made a good bargain when they have found anyone disposed to take care of the fruit which the ground supplies almost spontaneously in too great abundance, and for which there is no market. I felt compelled to admit the justice of the Romans who had called them Brutes instead of Byutians. The good priests with whom I had been travelling laughed at my dread of the tarantula and of the crasydra, for the disease brought on by the bite of those insects appeared to me more fearful even than a certain disease with which I was already too well acquainted. They assured me that all the stories relating to those creatures were fables; they laughed at the lines which Virgil has devoted to them in the Georgics as well as at all those I quoted to justify my fears.

I found Bishop Bernard de Bernardis occupying a hard chair near an old table on which he was writing. I fell on my knees, as it is customary to do before a prelate, but, instead of giving me his blessing, he raised me up from the floor, and, folding me in his arms, embraced me tenderly. He expressed his deep sorrow when I told him that in Naples I had not been able to find any instructions to enable me to join him, but his face lighted up again when I added that I was indebted to no one for money, and that I was in good health. He bade me take a seat, and with a heavy sigh he began to talk of his poverty, and ordered a servant to lay the cloth for three persons. Besides this servant, his lordship's suite consisted of a most devout-looking housekeeper, and of a priest whom I judged to be very ignorant from the few words he uttered during our meal. The house inhabited by his lordship was large, but badly built and poorly kept. The furniture was so miserable that, in order to make up a bed for me in the room adjoining his chamber, the poor bishop had to give up one of his two mattresses! His dinner, not to say any more about it, frightened me, for he was very strict in keeping the rules of his order, and this being a fast day, he did not eat any meat, and the oil was very bad. Nevertheless, monsignor was an intelligent man, and, what is still better, an honest man. He told me, much to my surprise, that his bishopric, although not one of little importance, brought him in only five hundred ducat-diregno yearly, and that, unfortunately, he had contracted debts to the amount of six hundred. He added, with a sigh, that his only happiness was to feel himself out of the clutches of the monks, who had persecuted him, and made his life a perfect purgatory for fifteen years. All these confidences caused me sorrow and mortification, because they proved to me, not only that I was not in the promised land where a mitre could be picked up, but also that I would be a heavy charge for him. I felt that he was grieved himself at the sorry present his patronage seemed likely to prove.

I enquired whether he had a good library, whether there were any literary men, or any good society in which one could spend a few agreeable hours. He smiled and answered that throughout his diocese there was not one man who could boast of writing decently, and still less of any taste or knowledge in literature; that there was not a single bookseller, nor any person caring even for the newspapers. But he promised me that we would follow our literary tastes together, as soon as he received the books he had ordered from Naples.

That was all very well, but was this the place for a young man of eighteen to live in, without a good library, without good society, without emulation and literacy intercourse? The good bishop, seeing me full of sad thoughts, and almost astounded at the prospect of the miserable life I should have to lead with him, tried to give me courage by promising to do everything in his power to secure my happiness.

The next day, the bishop having to officiate in his pontifical robes, I had an opportunity of seeing all the clergy, and all the faithful of the diocese, men and women, of whom the cathedral was full; the sight made me resolve at once to leave Martorano. I thought I was gazing upon a troop of brutes for whom my external appearance was a cause of scandal. How ugly were the women! What a look of stupidity and coarseness in the men! When I returned to the bishop's house I told the prelate that I did not feel in me the vocation to die within a few months a martyr in this miserable city.

"Give me your blessing," I added, "and let me go; or, rather, come with me. I promise you that we shall make a fortune somewhere else."

The proposal made him laugh repeatedly during the day. Had he agreed to it he would not have died two years afterwards in the prime of manhood. The worthy man, feeling how natural was my repugnance, begged me to forgive him for having summoned me to him, and, considering it his duty to send me back to Venice, having no money himself and not being aware that I had any, he told me that he would give me an introduction to a worthy citizen of Naples who would lend me sixty ducati-di-regno to enable me to reach my native city. I accepted his offer with gratitude, and going to my room I took out of my trunk the case of fine razors which the Greek had given me, and I begged his acceptance of it as a souvenir of me. I had great difficulty in forcing it upon him, for it was worth the sixty ducats, and to conquer his resistance I had to threaten to remain with him if he refused my present. He gave me a very flattering letter of recommendation for the Archbishop of Cosenza, in which he requested him to forward me as far as Naples without any expense to myself. It was thus I left Martorano sixty hours after my arrival, pitying the bishop whom I was leaving behind, and who wept as he was pouring heartfelt blessings upon me.

The Archbishop of Cosenza, a man of wealth and of intelligence, offered me a room in his palace. During the dinner I made, with an overflowing heart, the eulogy of the Bishop of Martorano; but I railed mercilessly at his diocese and at the whole of Calabria in so cutting a manner that I greatly amused the archbishop and all his guests, amongst whom were two ladies, his relatives, who did the honours of the dinner-table. The youngest, however, objected to the satirical style in which I had depicted her country, and declared war against me; but I contrived to obtain peace again by telling her that Calabria would be a delightful country if one-fourth only of its inhabitants were like her. Perhaps it was with the idea of proving to me that I had been wrong in my opinion that the archbishop gave on the following day a splendid supper.

Cosenza is a city in which a gentleman can find plenty of amusement; the nobility are wealthy, the women are pretty, and men generally well-informed, because they have been educated in Naples or in Rome. I left Cosenza on the third day with a letter from the archbishop for the far-famed Genovesi.

I had five travelling companions, whom I judged, from their appearance, to be either pirates or banditti, and I took very good care not to let them see or guess that I had a well-filled purse. I likewise thought it prudent to go to bed without undressing during the whole journey—an excellent measure of prudence for a young man travelling in that part of the country.

I reached Naples on the 16th of September, 1743, and I lost no time in presenting the letter of the Bishop of Martorano. It was addressed to a M. Gennaro Polo at St. Anne's. This excellent man, whose duty was only to give me the sum of sixty ducats, insisted, after perusing the bishop's letter, upon receiving me in his house, because he wished me to make the acquaintance of his son, who was a poet like myself. The bishop had represented my poetry as sublime. After the usual ceremonies, I accepted his kind invitation, my trunk was sent for, and I was a guest in the house of M. Gennaro Polo.

II

My Stay in Naples; It is Short but Happy—Don Antonio Casanova—Don Lelio Caraffa—I Go to Rome in Very Agreeable Company, and Enter the Service of Cardinal Acquaviva—Barbara—Testaccio—Frascati

I had no difficulty in answering the various questions which Doctor Gennaro addressed to me, but I was surprised, and even displeased, at the constant peals of laughter with which he received my answers. The piteous description of miserable Calabria, and the picture of the sad situation of the Bishop of Martorano, appeared to me more likely to call forth tears than to excite hilarity, and, suspecting that some mystification was being played upon me, I was very near getting angry when, becoming more composed, he told me with feeling that I must kindly excuse him; that his laughter was a disease which seemed to be endemic in his family, for one of his uncles died of it.

"What!" I exclaimed, "died of laughing!"

"Yes. This disease, which was not known to Hippocrates, is called li flati."

"What do you mean? Does an hypochondriac affection, which causes sadness and lowness in all those who suffer from it, render you cheerful?"

"Yes, because, most likely, my flati, instead of influencing the hypochondrium, affects my spleen, which my physician asserts to be the organ of laughter. It is quite a discovery."

"You are mistaken; it is a very ancient notion, and it is the only function which is ascribed to the spleen in our animal organization."

"Well, we must discuss the matter at length, for I hope you will remain with us a few weeks."

"I wish I could, but I must leave Naples to-morrow or the day after."

"Have you got any money?"

"I rely upon the sixty ducats you have to give me."

At these words, his peals of laughter began again, and as he could see that I was annoyed, he said, "I am amused at the idea that I can keep you here as long as I like. But be good enough to see my son; he writes pretty verses enough."

And truly his son, although only fourteen, was already a great poet.

A servant took me to the apartment of the young man whom I found possessed of a pleasing countenance and engaging manners. He gave me a polite welcome, and begged to be excused if he could not attend to me altogether for the present, as he had to finish a song which he was composing for a relative of the Duchess de Rovino, who was taking the veil at the Convent of St. Claire, and the printer was waiting for the manuscript. I told him that his excuse was a very good one, and I offered to assist him. He then read his song, and I found it so full of enthusiasm, and so truly in the style of Guidi, that I advised him to call it an ode; but as I had praised all the truly beautiful passages, I thought I could venture to point out the weak ones, and I replaced them by verses of my own composition. He was delighted, and thanked me warmly, inquiring whether I was Apollo. As he was writing his ode, I composed a sonnet on the same subject, and, expressing his admiration for it he begged me to sign it, and to allow him to send it with his poetry.

While I was correcting and recopying my manuscript, he went to his father to find out who I was, which made the old man laugh until supper-time. In the evening, I had the pleasure of seeing that my bed had been prepared in the young man's chamber.

Doctor Gennaro's family was composed of this son and of a daughter unfortunately very plain, of his wife and of two elderly, devout sisters. Amongst the guests at the supper-table I met several literary men, and the Marquis Galiani, who was at that time annotating Vitruvius. He had a brother, an abbe whose acquaintance I made twenty years after, in Paris, when he was secretary of embassy to Count Cantillana. The next day, at supper, I was presented to the celebrated Genovesi; I had already sent him the letter of the Archbishop of Cosenza. He spoke to me of Apostolo Zeno and of the Abbe Conti. He remarked that it was considered a very venial sin for a regular priest to say two masses in one day for the sake of earning two carlini more, but that for the same sin a secular priest would deserve to be burnt at the stake.

The nun took the veil on the following day, and Gennaro's ode and my sonnet had the greatest success. A Neapolitan gentleman, whose name was the same as mine, expressed a wish to know me, and, hearing that I resided at the doctor's, he called to congratulate him on the occasion of his feast-day, which happened to fall on the day following the ceremony at Sainte-Claire.

Don Antonio Casanova, informing me of his name, enquired whether my family was originally from Venice.

"I am, sir," I answered modestly, "the great-grandson of the unfortunate Marco Antonio Casanova, secretary to Cardinal Pompeo Colonna, who died of the plague in Rome, in the year 1528, under the pontificate of Clement VII." The words were scarcely out of my lips when he embraced me, calling me his cousin, but we all thought that Doctor Gennaro would actually die with laughter, for it seemed impossible to laugh so immoderately without risk of life. Madame Gennaro was very angry and told my newly-found cousin that he might have avoided enacting such a scene before her husband, knowing his disease, but he answered that he never thought the circumstance likely to provoke mirth. I said nothing, for, in reality, I felt that the recognition was very comic. Our poor laugher having recovered his composure, Casanova, who had remained very serious, invited me to dinner for the next day with my young friend Paul Gennaro, who had already become my alter ego.

When we called at his house, my worthy cousin showed me his family tree, beginning with a Don Francisco, brother of Don Juan. In my pedigree, which I knew by heart, Don Juan, my direct ancestor, was a posthumous child. It was possible that there might have been a brother of Marco Antonio's; but when he heard that my genealogy began with Don Francisco, from Aragon, who had lived in the fourteenth century, and that consequently all the pedigree of the illustrious house of the Casanovas of Saragossa belonged to him, his joy knew no bounds; he did not know what to do to convince me that the same blood was flowing in his veins and in mine.

He expressed some curiosity to know what lucky accident had brought me to Naples; I told him that, having embraced the ecclesiastical profession, I was going to Rome to seek my fortune. He then presented me to his family, and I thought that I could read on the countenance of my cousin, his dearly beloved wife, that she was not much pleased with the newly-found relationship, but his pretty daughter, and a still prettier niece of his, might very easily have given me faith in the doctrine that blood is thicker than water, however fabulous it may be.

After dinner, Don Antonio informed me that the Duchess de Bovino had expressed a wish to know the Abbe Casanova who had written the sonnet in honour of her relative, and that he would be very happy to introduce me to her as his own cousin. As we were alone at that moment, I begged he would not insist on presenting me, as I was only provided with travelling suits, and had to be careful of my purse so as not to arrive in Rome without money. Delighted at my confidence, and approving my economy, he said, "I am rich, and you must not scruple to come with me to my tailor;" and he accompanied his offer with an assurance that the circumstance would not be known to anyone, and that he would feel deeply mortified if I denied him the pleasure of serving me. I shook him warmly by the hand, and answered that I was ready to do anything he pleased. We went to a tailor who took my measure, and who brought me on the following day everything necessary to the toilet of the most elegant abbe. Don Antonio called on me, and remained to dine with Don Gennaro, after which he took me and my friend Paul to the duchess. This lady, according to the Neapolitan fashion, called me thou in her very first compliment of welcome. Her daughter, then only ten or twelve years old, was very handsome, and a few years later became Duchess de Matalona. The duchess presented me with a snuff-box in pale tortoise-shell with arabesque incrustations in gold, and she invited us to dine with her on the morrow, promising to take us after dinner to the Convent of St. Claire to pay a visit to the new nun.

As we came out of the palace of the duchess, I left my friends and went alone to Panagiotti's to claim the barrel of muscatel wine. The manager was kind enough to have the barrel divided into two smaller casks of equal capacity, and I sent one to Don Antonio, and the other to Don Gennaro. As I was leaving the shop I met the worthy Panagiotti, who was glad to see me. Was I to blush at the sight of the good man I had at first deceived? No, for in his opinion I had acted very nobly towards him.

Don Gennaro, as I returned home, managed to thank me for my handsome present without laughing, and the next day Don Antonio, to make up for the muscatel wine I had sent him, offered me a gold-headed cane, worth at least fifteen ounces, and his tailor brought me a travelling suit and a blue great coat, with the buttonholes in gold lace. I therefore found myself splendidly equipped.

At the Duchess de Bovino's dinner I made the acquaintance of the wisest and most learned man in Naples, the illustrious Don Lelio Caraffa, who belonged to the ducal family of Matalona, and whom King Carlos honoured with the title of friend.

I spent two delightful hours in the convent parlour, coping successfully with the curiosity of all the nuns who were pressing against the grating. Had destiny allowed me to remain in Naples my fortune would have been made; but, although I had no fixed plan, the voice of fate summoned me to Rome, and therefore I resisted all the entreaties of my cousin Antonio to accept the honourable position of tutor in several houses of the highest order.

Don Antonio gave a splendid dinner in my honour, but he was annoyed and angry because he saw that his wife looked daggers at her new cousin. I thought that, more than once, she cast a glance at my new costume, and then whispered to the guest next to her. Very likely she knew what had taken place. There are some positions in life to which I could never be reconciled. If, in the most brilliant circle, there is one person who affects to stare at me I lose all presence of mind. Self-dignity feels outraged, my wit dies away, and I play the part of a dolt. It is a weakness on my part, but a weakness I cannot overcome.

Don Lelio Caraffa offered me a very liberal salary if I would undertake the education of his nephew, the Duke de Matalona, then ten years of age. I expressed my gratitude, and begged him to be my true benefactor in a different manner—namely, by giving me a few good letters of introduction for Rome, a favour which he granted at once. He gave me one for Cardinal Acquaviva, and another for Father Georgi.

I found out that the interest felt towards me by my friends had induced them to obtain for me the honour of kissing the hand of Her Majesty the Queen, and I hastened my preparations to leave Naples, for the queen would certainly have asked me some questions, and I could not have avoided telling her that I had just left Martorano and the poor bishop whom she had sent there. The queen likewise knew my mother; she would very likely have alluded to my mother's profession in Dresden; it would have mortified Don Antonio, and my pedigree would have been covered with ridicule. I knew the force of prejudice! I should have been ruined, and I felt I should do well to withdraw in good time. As I took leave of him, Don Antonio presented me with a fine gold watch and gave me a letter for Don Gaspar Vidaldi, whom he called his best friend. Don Gennaro paid me the sixty ducats, and his son, swearing eternal friendship, asked me to write to him. They all accompanied me to the coach, blending their tears with mine, and loading me with good wishes and blessings.

From my landing in Chiozza up to my arrival in Naples, fortune had seemed bent upon frowning on me; in Naples it began to shew itself less adverse, and on my return to that city it entirely smiled upon me. Naples has always been a fortunate place for me, as the reader of my memoirs will discover. My readers must not forget that in Portici I was on the point of disgracing myself, and there is no remedy against the degradation of the mind, for nothing can restore it to its former standard. It is a case of disheartening atony for which there is no possible cure.

I was not ungrateful to the good Bishop of Martorano, for, if he had unwittingly injured me by summoning me to his diocese, I felt that to his letter for M. Gennaro I was indebted for all the good fortune which had just befallen me. I wrote to him from Rome.

I was wholly engaged in drying my tears as we were driving through the beautiful street of Toledo, and it was only after we had left Naples that I could find time to examine the countenance of my travelling companions. Next to me, I saw a man of from forty to fifty, with a pleasing face and a lively air, but, opposite to me, two charming faces delighted my eyes. They belonged to two ladies, young and pretty, very well dressed, with a look of candour and modesty. This discovery was most agreeable, but I felt sad and I wanted calm and silence. We reached Avessa without one word being exchanged, and as the vetturino stopped there only to water his mules, we did not get out of the coach. From Avessa to Capua my companions conversed almost without interruption, and, wonderful to relate! I did not open my lips once. I was amused by the Neapolitan jargon of the gentleman, and by the pretty accent of the ladies, who were evidently Romans. It was a most wonderful feat for me to remain five hours before two charming women without addressing one word to them, without paying them one compliment.

At Capua, where we were to spend the night, we put up at an inn, and were shown into a room with two beds—a very usual thing in Italy. The Neapolitan, addressing himself to me, said,

"Am I to have the honour of sleeping with the reverend gentleman?"

I answered in a very serious tone that it was for him to choose or to arrange it otherwise, if he liked. The answer made the two ladies smile, particularly the one whom I preferred, and it seemed to me a good omen.

We were five at supper, for it is usual for the vetturino to supply his travellers with their meals, unless some private agreement is made otherwise, and to sit down at table with them. In the desultory talk which went on during the supper, I found in my travelling companions decorum, propriety, wit, and the manners of persons accustomed to good society. I became curious to know who they were, and going down with the driver after supper, I asked him.

"The gentleman," he told me, "is an advocate, and one of the ladies is his wife, but I do not know which of the two."

I went back to our room, and I was polite enough to go to bed first, in order to make it easier for the ladies to undress themselves with freedom; I likewise got up first in the morning, left the room, and only returned when I was called for breakfast. The coffee was delicious. I praised it highly, and the lady, the one who was my favourite, promised that I should have the same every morning during our journey. The barber came in after breakfast; the advocate was shaved, and the barber offered me his services, which I declined, but the rogue declared that it was slovenly to wear one's beard.

When we had resumed our seats in the coach, the advocate made some remark upon the impudence of barbers in general.

"But we ought to decide first," said the lady, "whether or not it is slovenly to go bearded."

"Of course it is," said the advocate. "Beard is nothing but a dirty excrescence."

"You may think so," I answered, "but everybody does not share your opinion. Do we consider as a dirty excrescence the hair of which we take so much care, and which is of the same nature as the beard? Far from it; we admire the length and the beauty of the hair."

"Then," remarked the lady, "the barber is a fool."

"But after all," I asked, "have I any beard?"

"I thought you had," she answered.

"In that case, I will begin to shave as soon as I reach Rome, for this is the first time that I have been convicted of having a beard."

"My dear wife," exclaimed the advocate, "you should have held your tongue; perhaps the reverend abbe is going to Rome with the intention of becoming a Capuchin friar."

The pleasantry made me laugh, but, unwilling that he should have the last word, I answered that he had guessed rightly, that such had been my intention, but that I had entirely altered my mind since I had seen his wife.

"Oh! you are wrong," said the joyous Neapolitan, "for my wife is very fond of Capuchins, and if you wish to please her, you had better follow your original vocation." Our conversation continued in the same tone of pleasantry, and the day passed off in an agreeable manner; in the evening we had a very poor supper at Garillan, but we made up for it by cheerfulness and witty conversation. My dawning inclination for the advocate's wife borrowed strength from the affectionate manner she displayed towards me.

The next day she asked me, after we had resumed our journey, whether I intended to make a long stay in Rome before returning to Venice. I answered that, having no acquaintances in Rome, I was afraid my life there would be very dull.

"Strangers are liked in Rome," she said, "I feel certain that you will be pleased with your residence in that city."

"May I hope, madam, that you will allow me to pay you my respects?"

"We shall be honoured by your calling on us," said the advocate.

My eyes were fixed upon his charming wife. She blushed, but I did not appear to notice it. I kept up the conversation, and the day passed as pleasantly as the previous one. We stopped at Terracina, where they gave us a room with three beds, two single beds and a large one between the two others. It was natural that the two sisters should take the large bed; they did so, and undressed themselves while the advocate and I went on talking at the table, with our backs turned to them. As soon as they had gone to rest, the advocate took the bed on which he found his nightcap, and I the other, which was only about one foot distant from the large bed. I remarked that the lady by whom I was captivated was on the side nearest my couch, and, without much vanity, I could suppose that it was not owing only to chance.

I put the light out and laid down, revolving in my mind a project which I could not abandon, and yet durst not execute. In vain did I court sleep. A very faint light enabled me to perceive the bed in which the pretty woman was lying, and my eyes would, in spite of myself, remain open. It would be difficult to guess what I might have done at last (I had already fought a hard battle with myself for more than an hour), when I saw her rise, get out of her bed, and go and lay herself down near her husband, who, most likely, did not wake up, and continued to sleep in peace, for I did not hear any noise.

Vexed, disgusted. . . I tried to compose myself to sleep, and I woke only at day-break. Seeing the beautiful wandering star in her own bed, I got up, dressed myself in haste, and went out, leaving all my companions fast asleep. I returned to the inn only at the time fixed for our departure, and I found the advocate and the two ladies already in the coach, waiting for me.

The lady complained, in a very obliging manner, of my not having cared for her coffee; I pleaded as an excuse a desire for an early walk, and I took care not to honour her even with a look; I feigned to be suffering from the toothache, and remained in my corner dull and silent. At Piperno she managed to whisper to me that my toothache was all sham; I was pleased with the reproach, because it heralded an explanation which I craved for, in spite of my vexation.

During the afternoon I continued my policy of the morning. I was morose and silent until we reached Serinonetta, where we were to pass the night. We arrived early, and the weather being fine, the lady said that she could enjoy a walk, and asked me politely to offer her my arm. I did so, for it would have been rude to refuse; besides I had had enough of my sulking fit. An explanation could alone bring matters back to their original standing, but I did not know how to force it upon the lady. Her husband followed us at some distance with the sister.

When we were far enough in advance, I ventured to ask her why she had supposed my toothache to have been feigned.

"I am very candid," she said; "it is because the difference in your manner was so marked, and because you were so careful to avoid looking at me through the whole day. A toothache would not have prevented you from being polite, and therefore I thought it had been feigned for some purpose. But I am certain that not one of us can possibly have given you any grounds for such a rapid change in your manner."

"Yet something must have caused the change, and you, madam, are only half sincere."

"You are mistaken, sir, I am entirely sincere; and if I have given you any motive for anger, I am, and must remain, ignorant of it. Be good enough to tell me what I have done."

"Nothing, for I have no right to complain."

"Yes, you have; you have a right, the same that I have myself; the right which good society grants to every one of its members. Speak, and shew yourself as sincere as I am."

"You are certainly bound not to know, or to pretend not to know the real cause, but you must acknowledge that my duty is to remain silent."

"Very well; now it is all over; but if your duty bids you to conceal the cause of your bad humour, it also bids you not to shew it. Delicacy sometimes enforces upon a polite gentleman the necessity of concealing certain feelings which might implicate either himself or others; it is a restraint for the mind, I confess, but it has some advantage when its effect is to render more amiable the man who forces himself to accept that restraint." Her close argument made me blush for shame, and carrying her beautiful hand to my lips, I confessed my self in the wrong.

"You would see me at your feet," I exclaimed, "in token of my repentance, were I not afraid of injuring you—"

"Do not let us allude to the matter any more," she answered.

And, pleased with my repentance, she gave me a look so expressive of forgiveness that, without being afraid of augmenting my guilt, I took my lips off her hand and I raised them to her half-open, smiling mouth. Intoxicated with rapture, I passed so rapidly from a state of sadness to one of overwhelming cheerfulness that during our supper the advocate enjoyed a thousand jokes upon my toothache, so quickly cured by the simple remedy of a walk. On the following day we dined at Velletri and slept in Marino, where, although the town was full of troops, we had two small rooms and a good supper. I could not have been on better terms with my charming Roman; for, although I had received but a rapid proof of her regard, it had been such a true one—such a tender one! In the coach our eyes could not say much; but I was opposite to her, and our feet spoke a very eloquent language.

The advocate had told me that he was going to Rome on some ecclesiastical business, and that he intended to reside in the house of his mother-in-law, whom his wife had not seen since her marriage, two years ago, and her sister hoped to remain in Rome, where she expected to marry a clerk at the Spirito Santo Bank. He gave me their address, with a pressing invitation to call upon them, and I promised to devote all my spare time to them.

We were enjoying our dessert, when my beautiful lady-love, admiring my snuff-box, told her husband that she wished she had one like it.

"I will buy you one, dear."

"Then buy mine," I said; "I will let you have it for twenty ounces, and you can give me a note of hand payable to bearer in payment. I owe that amount to an Englishman, and I will give it him to redeem my debt."

"Your snuff-box, my dear abbe, is worth twenty ounces, but I cannot buy it unless you agree to receive payment in cash; I should be delighted to see it in my wife's possession, and she would keep it as a remembrance of you."

His wife, thinking that I would not accept his offer, said that she had no objection to give me the note of hand.

"But," exclaimed the advocate, "can you not guess the Englishman exists only in our friend's imagination? He would never enter an appearance, and we would have the snuff-box for nothing. Do not trust the abbe, my dear, he is a great cheat."

"I had no idea," answered his wife, looking at me, "that the world contained rogues of this species."

I affected a melancholy air, and said that I only wished myself rich enough to be often guilty of such cheating.

When a man is in love very little is enough to throw him into despair, and as little to enhance his joy to the utmost. There was but one bed in the room where supper had been served, and another in a small closet leading out of the room, but without a door. The ladies chose the closet, and the advocate retired to rest before me. I bid the ladies good night as soon as they had gone to bed; I looked at my dear mistress, and after undressing myself I went to bed, intending not to sleep through the night. But the reader may imagine my rage when I found, as I got into the bed, that it creaked loud enough to wake the dead. I waited, however, quite motionless, until my companion should be fast asleep, and as soon as his snoring told me that he was entirely under the influence of Morpheus, I tried to slip out of the bed; but the infernal creaking which took place whenever I moved, woke my companion, who felt about with his hand, and, finding me near him, went to sleep again. Half an hour after, I tried a second time, but with the same result. I had to give it up in despair.

Love is the most cunning of gods; in the midst of obstacles he seems to be in his own element, but as his very existence depends upon the enjoyment of those who ardently worship him, the shrewd, all-seeing, little blind god contrives to bring success out of the most desperate case.

I had given up all hope for the night, and had nearly gone to sleep, when suddenly we hear a dreadful noise. Guns are fired in the street, people, screaming and howling, are running up and down the stairs; at last there is a loud knocking at our door. The advocate, frightened out of his slumbers, asks me what it can all mean; I pretend to be very indifferent, and beg to be allowed to sleep. But the ladies are trembling with fear, and loudly calling for a light. I remain very quiet, the advocate jumps out of bed, and runs out of the room to obtain a candle; I rise at once, I follow him to shut the door, but I slam it rather too hard, the double spring of the lock gives way, and the door cannot be reopened without the key.

I approach the ladies in order to calm their anxiety, telling them that the advocate would soon return with a light, and that we should then know the cause of the tumult, but I am not losing my time, and am at work while I am speaking. I meet with very little opposition, but, leaning rather too heavily upon my fair lady, I break through the bottom of the bedstead, and we suddenly find ourselves, the two ladies and myself, all together in a heap on the floor. The advocate comes back and knocks at the door; the sister gets up, I obey the prayers of my charming friend, and, feeling my way, reach the door, and tell the advocate that I cannot open it, and that he must get the key. The two sisters are behind me. I extend my hand; but I am abruptly repulsed, and judge that I have addressed myself to the wrong quarter; I go to the other side, and there I am better received. But the husband returns, the noise of the key in the lock announces that the door is going to be opened, and we return to our respective beds.

The advocate hurries to the bed of the two frightened ladies, thinking of relieving their anxiety, but, when he sees them buried in their broken-down bedstead, he bursts into a loud laugh. He tells me to come and have a look at them, but I am very modest, and decline the invitation. He then tells us that the alarm has been caused by a German detachment attacking suddenly the Spanish troops in the city, and that the Spaniards are running away. In a quarter of an hour the noise has ceased, and quiet is entirely re-established.

The advocate complimented me upon my coolness, got into bed again, and was soon asleep. As for me, I was careful not to close my eyes, and as soon as I saw daylight I got up in order to perform certain ablutions and to change my shirt; it was an absolute necessity.

I returned for breakfast, and while we were drinking the delicious coffee which Donna Lucrezia had made, as I thought, better than ever, I remarked that her sister frowned on me. But how little I cared for her anger when I saw the cheerful, happy countenance, and the approving looks of my adored Lucrezia! I felt a delightful sensation run through the whole of my body.

We reached Rome very early. We had taken breakfast at the Tour, and the advocate being in a very gay mood I assumed the same tone, loading him with compliments, and predicting that a son would be born to him, I compelled his wife to promise it should be so. I did not forget the sister of my charming Lucrezia, and to make her change her hostile attitude towards me I addressed to her so many pretty compliments, and behaved in such a friendly manner, that she was compelled to forgive the fall of the bed. As I took leave of them, I promised to give them a call on the following day.

I was in Rome! with a good wardrobe, pretty well supplied with money and jewellery, not wanting in experience, and with excellent letters of introduction. I was free, my own master, and just reaching the age in which a man can have faith in his own fortune, provided he is not deficient in courage, and is blessed with a face likely to attract the sympathy of those he mixes with. I was not handsome, but I had something better than beauty—a striking expression which almost compelled a kind interest in my favour, and I felt myself ready for anything. I knew that Rome is the one city in which a man can begin from the lowest rung, and reach the very top of the social ladder. This knowledge increased my courage, and I must confess that a most inveterate feeling of self-esteem which, on account of my inexperience, I could not distrust, enhanced wonderfully my confidence in myself.

The man who intends to make his fortune in this ancient capital of the world must be a chameleon susceptible of reflecting all the colours of the atmosphere that surrounds him—a Proteus apt to assume every form, every shape. He must be supple, flexible, insinuating; close, inscrutable, often base, sometimes sincere, some times perfidious, always concealing a part of his knowledge, indulging in one tone of voice, patient, a perfect master of his own countenance as cold as ice when any other man would be all fire; and if unfortunately he is not religious at heart—a very common occurrence for a soul possessing the above requisites—he must have religion in his mind, that is to say, on his face, on his lips, in his manners; he must suffer quietly, if he be an honest man the necessity of knowing himself an arrant hypocrite. The man whose soul would loathe such a life should leave Rome and seek his fortune elsewhere. I do not know whether I am praising or excusing myself, but of all those qualities I possessed but one—namely, flexibility; for the rest, I was only an interesting, heedless young fellow, a pretty good blood horse, but not broken, or rather badly broken; and that is much worse.

I began by delivering the letter I had received from Don Lelio for Father Georgi. The learned monk enjoyed the esteem of everyone in Rome, and the Pope himself had a great consideration for him, because he disliked the Jesuits, and did not put a mask on to tear the mask from their faces, although they deemed themselves powerful enough to despise him.

He read the letter with great attention, and expressed himself disposed to be my adviser; and that consequently I might make him responsible for any evil which might befall me, as misfortune is not to be feared by a man who acts rightly. He asked me what I intended to do in Rome, and I answered that I wished him to tell me what to do.

"Perhaps I may; but in that case you must come and see me often, and never conceal from me anything, you understand, not anything, of what interests you, or of what happens to you."

"Don Lelio has likewise given me a letter for the Cardinal Acquaviva."

"I congratulate you; the cardinal's influence in Rome is greater even than that of the Pope."

"Must I deliver the letter at once?"

"No; I will see him this evening, and prepare him for your visit. Call on me to-morrow morning, and I will then tell you where and when you are to deliver your letter to the cardinal. Have you any money?"

"Enough for all my wants during one year."

"That is well. Have you any acquaintances?"

"Not one."

"Do not make any without first consulting me, and, above all, avoid coffee-houses and ordinaries, but if you should happen to frequent such places, listen and never speak. Be careful to form your judgment upon those who ask any questions from you, and if common civility obliges you to give an answer, give only an evasive one, if any other is likely to commit you. Do you speak French?"

"Not one word."

"I am sorry for that; you must learn French. Have you been a student?"

"A poor one, but I have a sufficient smattering to converse with ordinary company."

"That is enough; but be very prudent, for Rome is the city in which smatterers unmask each other, and are always at war amongst themselves. I hope you will take your letter to the cardinal, dressed like a modest abbe, and not in this elegant costume which is not likely to conjure fortune. Adieu, let me see you to-morrow."

Highly pleased with the welcome I had received at his hands, and with all he had said to me, I left his house and proceeded towards Campo-di-Fiore to deliver the letter of my cousin Antonio to Don Gaspar Vivaldi, who received me in his library, where I met two respectable-looking priests. He gave me the most friendly welcome, asked for my address, and invited me to dinner for the next day. He praised Father Georgi most highly, and, accompanying me as far as the stairs, he told me that he would give me on the morrow the amount his friend Don Antonio requested him to hand me.

More money which my generous cousin was bestowing on me! It is easy enough to give away when one possesses sufficient means to do it, but it is not every man who knows how to give. I found the proceeding of Don Antonio more delicate even than generous; I could not refuse his present; it was my duty to prove my gratitude by accepting it.

Just after I had left M. Vivaldi's house I found myself face to face with Stephano, and this extraordinary original loaded me with friendly caresses. I inwardly despised him, yet I could not feel hatred for him; I looked upon him as the instrument which Providence had been pleased to employ in order to save me from ruin. After telling me that he had obtained from the Pope all he wished, he advised me to avoid meeting the fatal constable who had advanced me two sequins in Seraval, because he had found out that I had deceived him, and had sworn revenge against me. I asked Stephano to induce the man to leave my acknowledgement of the debt in the hands of a certain merchant whom we both knew, and that I would call there to discharge the amount. This was done, and it ended the affair.

That evening I dined at the ordinary, which was frequented by Romans and foreigners; but I carefully followed the advice of Father Georgi. I heard a great deal of harsh language used against the Pope and against the Cardinal Minister, who had caused the Papal States to be inundated by eighty thousand men, Germans as well as Spaniards. But I was much surprised when I saw that everybody was eating meat, although it was Saturday. But a stranger during the first few days after his arrival in Rome is surrounded with many things which at first cause surprise, and to which he soon gets accustomed. There is not a Catholic city in the world in which a man is half so free on religious matters as in Rome. The inhabitants of Rome are like the men employed at the Government tobacco works, who are allowed to take gratis as much tobacco as they want for their own use. One can live in Rome with the most complete freedom, except that the 'ordini santissimi' are as much to be dreaded as the famous Lettres-de-cachet before the Revolution came and destroyed them, and shewed the whole world the general character of the French nation.

The next day, the 1st of October, 1743, I made up my mind to be shaved. The down on my chin had become a beard, and I judged that it was time to renounce some of the privileges enjoyed by adolescence.

I dressed myself completely in the Roman fashion, and Father Georgi was highly pleased when he saw me in that costume, which had been made by the tailor of my dear cousin, Don Antonio.

Father Georgi invited me to take a cup of chocolate with him, and informed me that the cardinal had been apprised of my arrival by a letter from Don Lelio, and that his eminence would receive me at noon at the Villa Negroni, where he would be taking a walk. I told Father Georgi that I had been invited to dinner by M. Vivaldi, and he advised me to cultivate his acquaintance.

I proceeded to the Villa Negroni; the moment he saw me the cardinal stopped to receive my letter, allowing two persons who accompanied him to walk forward. He put the letter in his pocket without reading it, examined me for one or two minutes, and enquired whether I felt any taste for politics. I answered that, until now, I had not felt in me any but frivolous tastes, but that I would make bold to answer for my readiness to execute all the orders which his eminence might be pleased to lay upon me, if he should judge me worthy of entering his service.

"Come to my office to-morrow morning," said the cardinal, "and ask for the Abbe Gama, to whom I will give my instructions. You must apply yourself diligently to the study of the French language; it is indispensable." He then enquired after Don Leilo's health, and after kissing his hand I took my leave.

I hastened to the house of M. Gaspar Vivaldi, where I dined amongst a well-chosen party of guests. M. Vivaldi was not married; literature was his only passion. He loved Latin poetry even better than Italian, and Horace, whom I knew by heart, was his favourite poet. After dinner, we repaired to his study, and he handed me one hundred Roman crowns, and Don Antonio's present, and assured me that I would be most welcome whenever I would call to take a cup of chocolate with him.

After I had taken leave of Don Gaspar, I proceeded towards the Minerva, for I longed to enjoy the surprise of my dear Lucrezia and of her sister; I inquired for Donna Cecilia Monti, their mother, and I saw, to my great astonishment, a young widow who looked like the sister of her two charming daughters. There was no need for me to give her my name; I had been announced, and she expected me. Her daughters soon came in, and their greeting caused me some amusement, for I did not appear to them to be the same individual. Donna Lucrezia presented me to her youngest sister, only eleven years of age, and to her brother, an abbe of fifteen, of charming appearance. I took care to behave so as to please the mother; I was modest, respectful, and shewed a deep interest in everything I saw. The good advocate arrived, and was surprised at the change in my appearance. He launched out in his usual jokes, and I followed him on that ground, yet I was careful not to give to my conversation the tone of levity which used to cause so much mirth in our travelling coach; so that, to, pay me a compliment, he told nee that, if I had had the sign of manhood shaved from my face, I had certainly transferred it to my mind. Donna Lucrezia did not know what to think of the change in my manners.

Towards evening I saw, coming in rapid succession, five or six ordinary-looking ladies, and as many abbes, who appeared to me some of the volumes with which I was to begin my Roman education. They all listened attentively to the most insignificant word I uttered, and I was very careful to let them enjoy their conjectures about me. Donna Cecilia told the advocate that he was but a poor painter, and that his portraits were not like the originals; he answered that she could not judge, because the original was shewing under a mask, and I pretended to be mortified by his answer. Donna Lucrezia said that she found me exactly the same, and her sister was of opinion that the air of Rome gave strangers a peculiar appearance. Everybody applauded, and Angelique turned red with satisfaction. After a visit of four hours I bowed myself out, and the advocate, following me, told me that his mother-in-law begged me to consider myself as a friend of the family, and to be certain of a welcome at any hour I liked to call. I thanked him gratefully and took my leave, trusting that I had pleased this amiable society as much as it had pleased me.

The next day I presented myself to the Abbe Gama. He was a Portuguese, about forty years old, handsome, and with a countenance full of candour, wit, and good temper. His affability claimed and obtained confidence. His manners and accent were quite Roman. He informed me, in the blandest manner, that his eminence had himself given his instructions about me to his majordomo, that I would have a lodging in the cardinal's palace, that I would have my meals at the secretaries' table, and that, until I learned French, I would have nothing to do but make extracts from letters that he would supply me with. He then gave me the address of the French teacher to whom he had already spoken in my behalf. He was a Roman advocate, Dalacqua by name, residing precisely opposite the palace.

After this short explanation, and an assurance that I could at all times rely upon his friendship, he had me taken to the major-domo, who made me sign my name at the bottom of a page in a large book, already filled with other names, and counted out sixty Roman crowns which he paid me for three months salary in advance. After this he accompanied me, followed by a 'staffiere' to my apartment on the third floor, which I found very comfortably furnished. The servant handed me the key, saying that he would come every morning to attend upon me, and the major-domo accompanied me to the gate to make me known to the gate-keeper. I immediately repaired to my inn, sent my luggage to the palace, and found myself established in a place in which a great fortune awaited me, if I had only been able to lead a wise and prudent life, but unfortunately it was not in my nature. 'Volentem ducit, nolentem trahit.'

I naturally felt it my duty to call upon my mentor, Father Georgi, to whom I gave all my good news. He said I was on the right road, and that my fortune was in my hands.

"Recollect," added the good father, "that to lead a blameless life you must curb your passions, and that whatever misfortune may befall you it cannot be ascribed by any one to a want of good luck, or attributed to fate; those words are devoid of sense, and all the fault will rightly fall on your own head."

"I foresee, reverend father, that my youth and my want of experience will often make it necessary for me to disturb you. I am afraid of proving myself too heavy a charge for you, but you will find me docile and obedient."

"I suppose you will often think me rather too severe; but you are not likely to confide everything to me."

"Everything, without any exception."

"Allow me to feel somewhat doubtful; you have not told me where you spent four hours yesterday."

"Because I did not think it was worth mentioning. I made the acquaintance of those persons during my journey; I believe them to be worthy and respectable, and the right sort of people for me to visit, unless you should be of a different opinion."

"God forbid! It is a very respectable house, frequented by honest people. They are delighted at having made your acquaintance; you are much liked by everybody, and they hope to retain you as a friend; I have heard all about it this morning; but you must not go there too often and as a regular guest."

"Must I cease my visits at once, and without cause?"

"No, it would be a want of politeness on your part. You may go there once or twice every week, but do not be a constant visitor. You are sighing, my son?"

"No, I assure you not. I will obey you."

"I hope it may not be only a matter of obedience, and I trust your heart will not feel it a hardship, but, if necessary, your heart must be conquered. Recollect that the heart is the greatest enemy of reason."

"Yet they can be made to agree."

"We often imagine so; but distrust the animism of your dear Horace. You know that there is no middle course with it: 'nisi paret, imperat'."

"I know it, but in the family of which we were speaking there is no danger for my heart."

"I am glad of it, because in that case it will be all the easier for you to abstain from frequent visits. Remember that I shall trust you."

"And I, reverend father; will listen to and follow your good advice. I will visit Donna Cecilia only now and then." Feeling most unhappy, I took his hand to press it against my lips, but he folded me in his arms as a father might have done, and turned himself round so as not to let me see that he was weeping.

I dined at the cardinal's palace and sat near the Abbe Gama; the table was laid for twelve persons, who all wore the costume of priests, for in Rome everyone is a priest or wishes to be thought a priest and as there is no law to forbid anyone to dress like an ecclesiastic that dress is adopted by all those who wish to be respected (noblemen excepted) even if they are not in the ecclesiastical profession.

I felt very miserable, and did not utter a word during the dinner; my silence was construed into a proof of my sagacity. As we rose from the table, the Abbe Gama invited me to spend the day with him, but I declined under pretence of letters to be written, and I truly did so for seven hours. I wrote to Don Lelio, to Don Antonio, to my young friend Paul, and to the worthy Bishop of Martorano, who answered that he heartily wished himself in my place.

Deeply enamoured of Lucrezia and happy in my love, to give her up appeared to me a shameful action. In order to insure the happiness of my future life, I was beginning to be the executioner of my present felicity, and the tormentor of my heart. I revolted against such a necessity which I judged fictitious, and which I could not admit unless I stood guilty of vileness before the tribunal of my own reason. I thought that Father Georgi, if he wished to forbid my visiting that family, ought not to have said that it was worthy of respect; my sorrow would not have been so intense. The day and the whole of the night were spent in painful thoughts.

In the morning the Abbe Gama brought me a great book filled with ministerial letters from which I was to compile for my amusement. After a short time devoted to that occupation, I went out to take my first French lesson, after which I walked towards the Strada-Condotta. I intended to take a long walk, when I heard myself called by my name. I saw the Abbe Gama in front of a coffee-house. I whispered to him that Minerva had forbidden me the coffee-rooms of Rome. "Minerva," he answered, "desires you to form some idea of such places. Sit down by me."

I heard a young abbe telling aloud, but without bitterness, a story, which attacked in a most direct manner the justice of His Holiness. Everybody was laughing and echoing the story. Another, being asked why he had left the services of Cardinal B., answered that it was because his eminence did not think himself called upon to pay him apart for certain private services, and everybody laughed outright. Another came to the Abbe Gama, and told him that, if he felt any inclination to spend the afternoon at the Villa Medicis, he would find him there with two young Roman girls who were satisfied with a 'quartino', a gold coin worth one-fourth of a sequin. Another abbe read an incendiary sonnet against the government, and several took a copy of it. Another read a satire of his own composition, in which he tore to pieces the honour of a family. In the middle of all that confusion, I saw a priest with a very attractive countenance come in. The size of his hips made me take him for a woman dressed in men's clothes, and I said so to Gama, who told me that he was the celebrated castrato, Bepino delta Mamana. The abbe called him to us, and told him with a laugh that I had taken him for a girl. The impudent fellow looked me full in the face, and said that, if I liked, he would shew me whether I had been right or wrong.

At the dinner-table everyone spoke to me, and I fancied I had given proper answers to all, but, when the repast was over, the Abbe Gama invited me to take coffee in his own apartment. The moment we were alone, he told me that all the guests I had met were worthy and honest men, and he asked me whether I believed that I had succeeded in pleasing the company.

"I flatter myself I have," I answered.

"You are wrong," said the abbe, "you are flattering yourself. You have so conspicuously avoided the questions put to you that everybody in the room noticed your extreme reserve. In the future no one will ask you any questions."

"I should be sorry if it should turn out so, but was I to expose my own concerns?"

"No, but there is a medium in all things."

"Yes, the medium of Horace, but it is often a matter of great difficulty to hit it exactly."

"A man ought to know how to obtain affection and esteem at the same time."

"That is the very wish nearest to my heart."

"To-day you have tried for the esteem much more than for the affection of your fellow-creatures. It may be a noble aspiration, but you must prepare yourself to fight jealousy and her daughter, calumny; if those two monsters do not succeed in destroying you, the victory must be yours. Now, for instance, you thoroughly refuted Salicetti to-day. Well, he is a physician, and what is more a Corsican; he must feel badly towards you."

"Could I grant that the longings of women during their pregnancy have no influence whatever on the skin of the foetus, when I know the reverse to be the case? Are you not of my opinion?"

"I am for neither party; I have seen many children with some such marks, but I have no means of knowing with certainty whether those marks have their origin in some longing experienced by the mother while she was pregnant."

"But I can swear it is so."

"All the better for you if your conviction is based upon such evidence, and all the worse for Salicetti if he denies the possibility of the thing without certain authority. But let him remain in error; it is better thus than to prove him in the wrong and to make a bitter enemy of him."

In the evening I called upon Lucrezia. The family knew my success, and warmly congratulated me. Lucrezia told me that I looked sad, and I answered that I was assisting at the funeral of my liberty, for I was no longer my own master. Her husband, always fond of a joke, told her that I was in love with her, and his mother-in-law advised him not to show so much intrepidity. I only remained an hour with those charming persons, and then took leave of them, but the very air around me was heated by the flame within my breast. When I reached my room I began to write, and spent the night in composing an ode which I sent the next day to the advocate. I was certain that he would shew it to his wife, who loved poetry, and who did not yet know that I was a poet. I abstained from seeing her again for three or four days. I was learning French, and making extracts from ministerial letters.

His eminence was in the habit of receiving every evening, and his rooms were thronged with the highest nobility of Rome; I had never attended these receptions. The Abbe Gama told me that I ought to do so as well as he did, without any pretension. I followed his advice and went; nobody spoke to me, but as I was unknown everyone looked at me and enquired who I was. The Abbe Gama asked me which was the lady who appeared to me the most amiable, and I shewed one to him; but I regretted having done so, for the courtier went to her, and of course informed her of what I had said. Soon afterwards I saw her look at me through her eye-glass and smile kindly upon me. She was the Marchioness G——, whose 'cicisbeo' was Cardinal S—— C——.

On the very day I had fixed to spend the evening with Donna Lucrezia the worthy advocate called upon me. He told me that if I thought I was going to prove I was not in love with his wife by staying away I was very much mistaken, and he invited me to accompany all the family to Testaccio, where they intended to have luncheon on the following Thursday. He added that his wife knew my ode by heart, and that she had read it to the intended husband of Angelique, who had a great wish to make my acquaintance. That gentleman was likewise a poet, and would be one of the party to Testaccio. I promised the advocate I would come to his house on the Thursday with a carriage for two.

At that time every Thursday in the month of October was a festival day in Rome. I went to see Donna Cecilia in the evening, and we talked about the excursion the whole time. I felt certain that Donna Lucrezia looked forward to it with as much pleasure as I did myself. We had no fixed plan, we could not have any, but we trusted to the god of love, and tacitly placed our confidence in his protection.

I took care that Father Georgi should not hear of that excursion before I mentioned it to him myself, and I hastened to him in order to obtain his permission to go. I confess that, to obtain his leave, I professed the most complete indifference about it, and the consequence was that the good man insisted upon my going, saying that it was a family party, and that it was quite right for me to visit the environs of Rome and to enjoy myself in a respectable way.

I went to Donna Cecilia's in a carriage which I hired from a certain Roland, a native of Avignon, and if I insist here upon his name it is because my readers will meet him again in eighteen years, his acquaintance with me having had very important results. The charming widow introduced me to Don Francisco, her intended son-in-law, whom she represented as a great friend of literary men, and very deeply learned himself. I accepted it as gospel, and behaved accordingly; yet I thought he looked rather heavy and not sufficiently elated for a young man on the point of marrying such a pretty girl as Angelique. But he had plenty of good-nature and plenty of money, and these are better than learning and gallantry.

As we were ready to get into the carriages, the advocate told me that he would ride with me in my carriage, and that the three ladies would go with Don Francisco in the other. I answered at once that he ought to keep Don Francisco company, and that I claimed the privilege of taking care of Donna Cecilia, adding that I should feel dishonoured if things were arranged differently. Thereupon I offered my arm to the handsome widow, who thought the arrangement according to the rules of etiquette and good breeding, and an approving look of my Lucrezia gave me the most agreeable sensation. Yet the proposal of the advocate struck me somewhat unpleasantly, because it was in contradiction with his former behaviour, and especially with what he had said to me in my room a few days before. "Has he become jealous?" I said to myself; that would have made me almost angry, but the hope of bringing him round during our stay at Testaccio cleared away the dark cloud on my mind, and I was very amiable to Donna Cecilia. What with lunching and walking we contrived to pass the afternoon very pleasantly; I was very gay, and my love for Lucrezia was not once mentioned; I was all attention to her mother. I occasionally addressed myself to Lucrezia, but not once to the advocate, feeling this the best way to shew him that he had insulted me.

As we prepared to return, the advocate carried off Donna Cecilia and went with her to the carriage in which were already seated Angelique and Don Francisco. Scarcely able to control my delight, I offered my arm to Donna Lucrezia, paying her some absurd compliment, while the advocate laughed outright, and seemed to enjoy the trick he imagined he had played me.

How many things we might have said to each other before giving ourselves up to the material enjoyment of our love, had not the instants been so precious! But, aware that we had only half an hour before us, we were sparing of the minutes. We were absorbed in voluptuous pleasure when suddenly Lucrezia exclaims,—

"Oh! dear, how unhappy we are!"

She pushes me back, composes herself, the carriage stops, and the servant opens the door. "What is the matter?" I enquire. "We are at home." Whenever I recollect the circumstance, it seems to me fabulous, for it is not possible to annihilate time, and the horses were regular old screws. But we were lucky all through. The night was dark, and my beloved angel happened to be on the right side to get out of the carriage first, so that, although the advocate was at the door of the brougham as soon as the footman, everything went right, owing to the slow manner in which Lucrezia alighted. I remained at Donna Cecilia's until midnight.

When I got home again, I went to bed; but how could I sleep? I felt burning in me the flame which I had not been able to restore to its original source in the too short distance from Testaccio to Rome. It was consuming me. Oh! unhappy are those who believe that the pleasures of Cythera are worth having, unless they are enjoyed in the most perfect accord by two hearts overflowing with love!

I only rose in time for my French lesson. My teacher had a pretty daughter, named Barbara, who was always present during my lessons, and who sometimes taught me herself with even more exactitude than her father. A good-looking young man, who likewise took lessons, was courting her, and I soon perceived that she loved him. This young man called often upon me, and I liked him, especially on account of his reserve, for, although I made him confess his love for Barbara, he always changed the subject, if I mentioned it in our conversation.

I had made up my mind to respect his reserve, and had not alluded to his affection for several days. But all at once I remarked that he had ceased his visits both to me and to his teacher, and at the same time I observed that the young girl was no longer present at my lessons; I felt some curiosity to know what had happened, although it was not, after all, any concern of mine.

A few days after, as I was returning from church, I met the young man, and reproached him for keeping away from us all. He told me that great sorrow had befallen him, which had fairly turned his brain, and that he was a prey to the most intense despair. His eyes were wet with tears. As I was leaving him, he held me back, and I told him that I would no longer be his friend unless he opened his heart to me. He took me to one of the cloisters, and he spoke thus:

"I have loved Barbara for the last six months, and for three months she has given me indisputable proofs of her affection. Five days ago, we were betrayed by the servant, and the father caught us in a rather delicate position. He left the room without saying one word, and I followed him, thinking of throwing myself at his feet; but, as I appeared before him, he took hold of me by the arm, pushed me roughly to the door, and forbade me ever to present myself again at his house. I cannot claim her hand in marriage, because one of my brothers is married, and my father is not rich; I have no profession, and my mistress has nothing. Alas, now that I have confessed all to you, tell me, I entreat you, how she is. I am certain that she is as miserable as I am myself. I cannot manage to get a letter delivered to her, for she does not leave the house, even to attend church. Unhappy wretch! What shall I do?"

I could but pity him, for, as a man of honour, it was impossible for me to interfere in such a business. I told him that I had not seen Barbara for five days, and, not knowing what to say, I gave him the advice which is tendered by all fools under similar circumstances; I advised him to forget his mistress.

We had then reached the quay of Ripetta, and, observing that he was casting dark looks towards the Tiber, I feared his despair might lead him to commit some foolish attempt against his own life, and, in order to calm his excited feelings, I promised to make some enquiries from the father about his mistress, and to inform him of all I heard. He felt quieted by my promise, and entreated me not to forget him.

In spite of the fire which had been raging through my veins ever since the excursion to Testaccio, I had not seen my Lucrezia for four days. I dreaded Father Georgi's suave manner, and I was still more afraid of finding he had made up his mind to give me no more advice. But, unable to resist my desires, I called upon Lucrezia after my French lesson, and found her alone, sad and dispirited.

"Ah!" she exclaimed, as soon as I was by her side, "I think you might find time to come and see me!"

"My beloved one, it is not that I cannot find time, but I am so jealous of my love that I would rather die than let it be known publicly. I have been thinking of inviting you all to dine with me at Frascati. I will send you a phaeton, and I trust that some lucky accident will smile upon our love."

"Oh! yes, do, dearest! I am sure your invitation will be accepted."

In a quarter of an hour the rest of the family came in, and I proffered my invitation for the following Sunday, which happened to be the Festival of St. Ursula, patroness of Lucrezia's youngest sister. I begged

Donna Cecilia to bring her as well as her son. My proposal being readily accepted, I gave notice that the phaeton would be at Donna Cecilia's door at seven o'clock, and that I would come myself with a carriage for two persons.

The next day I went to M. Dalacqua, and, after my lesson, I saw Barbara who, passing from one room to another, dropped a paper and earnestly looked at me. I felt bound to pick it up, because a servant, who was at hand, might have seen it and taken it. It was a letter, enclosing another addressed to her lover. The note for me ran thus: "If you think it to be a sin to deliver the enclosed to your friend, burn it. Have pity on an unfortunate girl, and be discreet."

The enclosed letter which was unsealed, ran as follows: "If you love me as deeply as 'I love you, you cannot hope to be happy without me; we cannot correspond in any other way than the one I am bold enough to adopt. I am ready to do anything to unite our lives until death. Consider and decide."

The cruel situation of the poor girl moved me almost to tears; yet I determined to return her letter the next day, and I enclosed it in a note in which I begged her to excuse me if I could not render her the service she required at my hands. I put it in my pocket ready for delivery. The next day I went for my lesson as usual, but, not seeing Barbara, I had no opportunity of returning her letter, and postponed its delivery to the following day. Unfortunately, just after I had returned to my room, the unhappy lover made his appearance. His eyes were red from weeping, his voice hoarse; he drew such a vivid picture of his misery, that, dreading some mad action counselled by despair, I could not withhold from him the consolation which I knew it was in my power to give. This was my first error in this fatal business; I was the victim of my own kindness.

The poor fellow read the letter over and over; he kissed it with transports of joy; he wept, hugged me, and thanked me for saving his life, and finally entreated me to take charge of his answer, as his beloved mistress must be longing for consolation as much as he had been himself, assuring me that his letter could not in any way implicate me, and that I was at liberty to read it.

And truly, although very long, his letter contained nothing but the assurance of everlasting love, and hopes which could not be realized. Yet I was wrong to accept the character of Mercury to the two young lovers. To refuse, I had only to recollect that Father Georgi would certainly have disapproved of my easy compliance.

The next day I found M. Dalacqua ill in bed; his daughter gave me my lesson in his room, and I thought that perhaps she had obtained her pardon. I contrived to give her her lover's letter, which she dextrously conveyed to her pocket, but her blushes would have easily betrayed her if her father had been looking that way. After the lesson I gave M. Dalacqua notice that I would not come on the morrow, as it was the Festival of St. Ursula, one of the eleven thousand princesses and martyr-virgins.

In the evening, at the reception of his eminence, which I attended regularly, although persons of distinction seldom spoke to me, the cardinal beckoned to me. He was speaking to the beautiful Marchioness G——, to whom Gama had indiscreetly confided that I thought her the handsomest woman amongst his eminence's guests.

"Her grace," said the Cardinal, "wishes to know whether you are making rapid progress in the French language, which she speaks admirably."

I answered in Italian that I had learned a great deal, but that I was not yet bold enough to speak.

"You should be bold," said the marchioness, "but without showing any pretension. It is the best way to disarm criticism."

My mind having almost unwittingly lent to the words "You should be bold" a meaning which had very likely been far from the idea of the marchioness, I turned very red, and the handsome speaker, observing it, changed the conversation and dismissed me.

The next morning, at seven o'clock, I was at Donna Cecilia's door. The phaeton was there as well as the carriage for two persons, which this time was an elegant vis-a-vis, so light and well-hung that Donna Cecilia praised it highly when she took her seat.

"I shall have my turn as we return to Rome," said Lucrezia; and I bowed to her as if in acceptance of her promise.

Lucrezia thus set suspicion at defiance in order to prevent suspicion arising. My happiness was assured, and I gave way to my natural flow of spirits. I ordered a splendid dinner, and we all set out towards the Villa Ludovisi. As we might have missed each other during our ramblings, we agreed to meet again at the inn at one o'clock. The discreet widow took the arm of her son-in-law, Angelique remained with her sister, and Lucrezia was my delightful share; Ursula and her brother were running about together, and in less than a quarter of an hour I had Lucrezia entirely to myself.

"Did you remark," she said, "with what candour I secured for us two hours of delightful 'tete-a-tete', and a 'tete-a-tete' in a 'vis-a-vis', too! How clever Love is!"

"Yes, darling, Love has made but one of our two souls. I adore you, and if I have the courage to pass so many days without seeing you it is in order to be rewarded by the freedom of one single day like this."

"I did not think it possible. But you have managed it all very well. You know too much for your age, dearest."

"A month ago, my beloved, I was but an ignorant child, and you are the first woman who has initiated me into the mysteries of love. Your departure will kill me, for I could not find another woman like you in all Italy."

"What! am I your first love? Alas! you will never be cured of it. Oh! why am I not entirely your own? You are also the first true love of my heart, and you will be the last. How great will be the happiness of my successor! I should not be jealous of her, but what suffering would be mine if I thought that her heart was not like mine!"

Lucrezia, seeing my eyes wet with tears, began to give way to her own, and, seating ourselves on the grass, our lips drank our tears amidst the sweetest kisses. How sweet is the nectar of the tears shed by love, when that nectar is relished amidst the raptures of mutual ardour! I have often tasted them—those delicious tears, and I can say knowingly that the ancient physicians were right, and that the modern are wrong.

In a moment of calm, seeing the disorder in which we both were, I told her that we might be surprised.

"Do not fear, my best beloved," she said, "we are under the guardianship of our good angels."

We were resting and reviving our strength by gazing into one another's eyes, when suddenly Lucrezia, casting a glance to the right, exclaimed,

"Look there! idol of my heart, have I not told you so? Yes, the angels are watching over us! Ah! how he stares at us! He seems to try to give us confidence. Look at that little demon; admire him! He must certainly be your guardian spirit or mine."

I thought she was delirious.

"What are you saying, dearest? I do not understand you. What am I to admire?"

"Do you not see that beautiful serpent with the blazing skin, which lifts its head and seems to worship us?"

I looked in the direction she indicated, and saw a serpent with changeable colours about three feet in length, which did seem to be looking at us. I was not particularly pleased at the sight, but I could not show myself less courageous than she was.

"What!" said I, "are you not afraid?"

"I tell you, again, that the sight is delightful to me, and I feel certain that it is a spirit with nothing but the shape, or rather the appearance, of a serpent."

"And if the spirit came gliding along the grass and hissed at you?"

"I would hold you tighter against my bosom, and set him at defiance. In your arms Lucrezia is safe. Look! the spirit is going away. Quick, quick! He is warning us of the approach of some profane person, and tells us to seek some other retreat to renew our pleasures. Let us go."

We rose and slowly advanced towards Donna Cecilia and the advocate, who were just emerging from a neighbouring alley. Without avoiding them, and without hurrying, just as if to meet one another was a very natural occurrence, I enquired of Donna Cecilia whether her daughter had any fear of serpents.

"In spite of all her strength of mind," she answered, "she is dreadfully afraid of thunder, and she will scream with terror at the sight of the smallest snake. There are some here, but she need not be frightened, for they are not venomous."

I was speechless with astonishment, for I discovered that I had just witnessed a wonderful love miracle. At that moment the children came up, and, without ceremony, we again parted company.

"Tell me, wonderful being, bewitching woman, what would you have done if, instead of your pretty serpent, you had seen your husband and your mother?"

"Nothing. Do you not know that, in moments of such rapture, lovers see and feel nothing but love? Do you doubt having possessed me wholly, entirely?"

Lucrezia, in speaking thus, was not composing a poetical ode; she was not feigning fictitious sentiments; her looks, the sound of her voice, were truth itself!

"Are you certain," I enquired, "that we are not suspected?"

"My husband does not believe us to be in love with each other, or else he does not mind such trifling pleasures as youth is generally wont to indulge in. My mother is a clever woman, and perhaps she suspects the truth, but she is aware that it is no longer any concern of hers. As to my sister, she must know everything, for she cannot have forgotten the broken-down bed; but she is prudent, and besides, she has taken it into her head to pity me. She has no conception of the nature of my feelings towards you. If I had not met you, my beloved, I should probably have gone through life without realizing such feelings myself; for what I feel for my husband. . . well, I have for him the obedience which my position as a wife imposes upon me."

"And yet he is most happy, and I envy him! He can clasp in his arms all your lovely person whenever he likes! There is no hateful veil to hide any of your charms from his gaze."

"Oh! where art thou, my dear serpent? Come to us, come and protect us against the surprise of the uninitiated, and this very instant I fulfil all the wishes of him I adore!"

We passed the morning in repeating that we loved each other, and in exchanging over and over again substantial proofs of our mutual passion.

We had a delicious dinner, during which I was all attention for the amiable Donna Cecilia. My pretty tortoise-shell box, filled with excellent snuff, went more than once round the table. As it happened to be in the hands of Lucrezia who was sitting on my left, her husband told her that, if I had no objection, she might give me her ring and keep the snuff-box in exchange. Thinking that the ring was not of as much value as my box, I immediately accepted, but I found the ring of greater value. Lucrezia would not, however, listen to anything on that subject. She put the box in her pocket, and thus compelled me to keep her ring.

Dessert was nearly over, the conversation was very animated, when suddenly the intended husband of Angelique claimed our attention for the reading of a sonnet which he had composed and dedicated to me. I thanked him, and placing the sonnet in my pocket promised to write one for him. This was not, however, what he wished; he expected that, stimulated by emulation, I would call for paper and pen, and sacrifice to Apollo hours which it was much more to my taste to employ in worshipping another god whom his cold nature knew only by name. We drank coffee, I paid the bill, and we went about rambling through the labyrinthine alleys of the Villa Aldobrandini.

What sweet recollections that villa has left in my memory! It seemed as if I saw my divine Lucrezia for the first time. Our looks were full of ardent love, our hearts were beating in concert with the most tender impatience, and a natural instinct was leading us towards a solitary asylum which the hand of Love seemed to have prepared on purpose for the mysteries of its secret worship. There, in the middle of a long avenue, and under a canopy of thick foliage, we found a wide sofa made of grass, and sheltered by a deep thicket; from that place our eyes could range over an immense plain, and view the avenue to such a distance right and left that we were perfectly secure against any surprise. We did not require to exchange one word at the sight of this beautiful temple so favourable to our love; our hearts spoke the same language.

Without a word being spoken, our ready hands soon managed to get rid of all obstacles, and to expose in a state of nature all the beauties which are generally veiled by troublesome wearing apparel. Two whole hours were devoted to the most delightful, loving ecstasies. At last we exclaimed together in mutual ecstasy, "O Love, we thank thee!"

We slowly retraced our steps towards the carriages, revelling in our intense happiness. Lucrezia informed me that Angelique's suitor was wealthy, that he owned a splendid villa at Tivoli, and that most likely he would invite us all to dine and pass the night there. "I pray the god of love," she added, "to grant us a night as beautiful as this day has been." Then, looking sad, she said, "But alas! the ecclesiastical lawsuit which has brought my husband to Rome is progressing so favourably that I am mortally afraid he will obtain judgment all too soon."

The journey back to the city lasted two hours; we were alone in my vis-a-vis and we overtaxed nature, exacting more than it can possibly give. As we were getting near Rome we were compelled to let the curtain fall before the denouement of the drama which we had performed to the complete satisfaction of the actors.

I returned home rather fatigued, but the sound sleep which was so natural at my age restored my full vigour, and in the morning I took my French lesson at the usual hour.

III

M. Dalacqua being very ill, his daughter Barbara gave me my lesson. When it was over, she seized an opportunity of slipping a letter into my pocket, and immediately disappeared, so that I had no chance of refusing. The letter was addressed to me, and expressed feelings of the warmest gratitude. She only desired me to inform her lover that her father had spoken to her again, and that most likely he would engage a new servant as soon as he had recovered from his illness, and she concluded her letter by assuring me that she never would implicate me in this business.

Her father was compelled to keep his bed for a fortnight, and Barbara continued to give me my lesson every day. I felt for her an interest which, from me towards a young and pretty girl, was, indeed, quite a new sentiment. It was a feeling of pity, and I was proud of being able to help and comfort her. Her eyes never rested upon mine, her hand never met mine, I never saw in her toilet the slightest wish to please me. She was very pretty, and I knew she had a tender, loving nature; but nothing interfered with the respect and the regard which I was bound in honour and in good faith to feel towards her, and I was proud to remark that she never thought me capable of taking advantage of her weakness or of her position.

When the father had recovered he dismissed his servant and engaged another. Barbara entreated me to inform her friend of the circumstance, and likewise of her hope to gain the new servant to their interests, at least sufficiently to secure the possibility of carrying on some correspondence. I promised to do so, and as a mark of her gratitude she took my hand to carry it to her lips, but quickly withdrawing it I tried to kiss her; she turned her face away, blushing deeply. I was much pleased with her modesty.

Barbara having succeeded in gaining the new servant over, I had nothing more to do with the intrigue, and I was very glad of it, for I knew my interference might have brought evil on my own head. Unfortunately, it was already too late.

I seldom visited Don Gaspar; the study of the French language took up all my mornings, and it was only in the morning that I could see him; but I called every evening upon Father Georgi, and, although I went to him only as one of his 'proteges', it gave me some reputation. I seldom spoke before his guests, yet I never felt weary, for in his circle his friends would criticise without slandering, discuss politics without stubbornness, literature without passion, and I profited by all. After my visit to the sagacious monk, I used to attend the assembly of the cardinal, my master, as a matter of duty. Almost every evening, when she happened to see me at her card-table, the beautiful marchioness would address to me a few gracious words in French, and I always answered in Italian, not caring to make her laugh before so many persons. My feelings for her were of a singular kind. I must leave them to the analysis of the reader. I thought that woman charming, yet I avoided her; it was not because I was afraid of falling in love with her; I loved Lucrezia, and I firmly believed that such an affection was a shield against any other attachment, but it was because I feared that she might love me or have a passing fancy for me. Was it self-conceit or modesty, vice or virtue? Perhaps neither one nor the other.

One evening she desired the Abbe Gama to call me to her; she was standing near the cardinal, my patron, and the moment I approached her she caused me a strange feeling of surprise by asking me in Italian a question which I was far from anticipating:

"How did you like Frascati?"

"Very much, madam; I have never seen such a beautiful place."

"But your company was still more beautiful, and your vis-a-vis was very smart."

I only bowed low to the marchioness, and a moment after Cardinal Acquaviva said to me, kindly,

"You are astonished at your adventure being known?"

"No, my lord; but I am surprised that people should talk of it. I could not have believed Rome to be so much like a small village."

"The longer you live in Rome," said his eminence, "the more you will find it so. You have not yet presented yourself to kiss the foot of our Holy Father?"

"Not yet, my lord."

"Then you must do so."

I bowed in compliance to his wishes.

The Abbe Gama told me to present myself to the Pope on the morrow, and he added,

"Of course you have already shewn yourself in the Marchioness G.'s palace?"

"No, I have never been there."

"You astonish me; but she often speaks to you!"

"I have no objection to go with you."

"I never visit at her palace."

"Yet she speaks to you likewise."

"Yes, but. . . You do not know Rome; go alone; believe me, you ought to go."

"Will she receive me?"

"You are joking, I suppose. Of course it is out of the question for you to be announced. You will call when the doors are wide open to everybody. You will meet there all those who pay homage to her."

"Will she see me?"

"No doubt of it."

On the following day I proceeded to Monte-Cavallo, and I was at once led into the room where the Pope was alone. I threw myself on my knees and kissed the holy cross on his most holy slipper. The Pope enquiring who I was, I told him, and he answered that he knew me, congratulating me upon my being in the service of so eminent a cardinal. He asked me how I had succeeded in gaining the cardinal's favour; I answered with a faithful recital of my adventures from my arrival at Martorano. He laughed heartily at all I said respecting the poor and worthy bishop, and remarked that, instead of trying to address him in Tuscan, I could speak in the Venetian dialect, as he was himself speaking to me in the dialect of Bologna. I felt quite at my ease with him, and I told him so much news and amused him so well that the Holy Father kindly said that he would be glad to see me whenever I presented myself at Monte-Cavallo. I begged his permission to read all forbidden books, and he granted it with his blessing, saying that I should have the permission in writing, but he forgot it.

Benedict XIV, was a learned man, very amiable, and fond of a joke. I saw him for the second time at the Villa Medicis. He called me to him, and continued his walk, speaking of trifling things. He was then accompanied by Cardinal Albani and the ambassador from Venice. A man of modest appearance approached His Holiness, who asked what he required; the man said a few words in a low voice, and, after listening to him, the Pope answered, "You are right, place your trust in God;" and he gave him his blessing. The poor fellow went away very dejected, and the Holy Father continued his walk.

"This man," I said, "most Holy Father, has not been pleased with the answer of Your Holiness."

"Why?"

"Because most likely he had already addressed himself to God before he ventured to apply to you; and when Your Holiness sends him to God again, he finds himself sent back, as the proverb says, from Herod to Pilate."

The Pope, as well as his two companions, laughed heartily; but I kept a serious countenance.

"I cannot," continued the Pope, "do any good without God's assistance."

"Very true, Holy Father; but the man is aware that you are God's prime minister, and it is easy to imagine his trouble now that the minister sends him again to the master. His only resource is to give money to the beggars of Rome, who for one 'bajocco' will pray for him. They boast of their influence before the throne of the Almighty, but as I have faith only in your credit, I entreat Your Holiness to deliver me of the heat which inflames my eyes by granting me permission to eat meat."

"Eat meat, my son."

"Holy Father, give me your blessing."

He blessed me, adding that I was not dispensed from fasting.

That very evening, at the cardinal's assembly, I found that the news of my dialogue with the Pope was already known. Everybody was anxious to speak to me. I felt flattered, but I was much more delighted at the joy which Cardinal Acquaviva tried in vain to conceal.

As I wished not to neglect Gama's advice, I presented myself at the mansion of the beautiful marchioness at the hour at which everyone had free access to her ladyship. I saw her, I saw the cardinal and a great many abbes; but I might have supposed myself invisible, for no one honoured me with a look, and no one spoke to me. I left after having performed for half an hour the character of a mute. Five or six days afterwards, the marchioness told me graciously that she had caught a sight of me in her reception-rooms.

"I was there, it is true, madam; but I had no idea that I had had the honour to be seen by your ladyship."

"Oh! I see everybody. They tell me that you have wit."

"If it is not a mistake on the part of your informants, your ladyship gives me very good news."

"Oh! they are excellent judges."

"Then, madam, those persons must have honoured me with their conversation; otherwise, it is not likely that they would have been able to express such an opinion."

"No doubt; but let me see you often at my receptions."

Our conversation had been overheard by those who were around; his excellency the cardinal told me that, when the marchioness addressed herself particularly to me in French, my duty was to answer her in the same language, good or bad. The cunning politician Gama took me apart, and remarked that my repartees were too smart, too cutting, and that, after a time, I would be sure to displease. I had made considerable progress in French; I had given up my lessons, and practice was all I required. I was then in the habit of calling sometimes upon Lucrezia in the morning, and of visiting in the evening Father Georgi, who was acquainted with the excursion to Frascati, and had not expressed any dissatisfaction.

Two days after the sort of command laid upon me by the marchioness, I presented myself at her reception. As soon as she saw me, she favoured me with a smile which I acknowledged by a deep reverence; that was all. In a quarter of an hour afterwards I left the mansion. The marchioness was beautiful, but she was powerful, and I could not make up my mind to crawl at the feet of power, and, on that head, I felt disgusted with the manners of the Romans.

One morning towards the end of November the advocate, accompanied by Angelique's intended, called on me. The latter gave me a pressing invitation to spend twenty-four hours at Tivoli with the friends I had entertained at Frascati. I accepted with great pleasure, for I had found no opportunity of being alone with Lucrezia since the Festival of St. Ursula. I promised to be at Donna Cecilia's house at day-break with the same 'is-a-vis'. It was necessary to start very early, because Tivoli is sixteen miles from Rome, and has so many objects of interest that it requires many hours to see them all. As I had to sleep out that night, I craved permission to do so from the cardinal himself, who, hearing with whom I was going, told me that I was quite right not to lose such an opportunity of visiting that splendid place in such good society.

The first dawn of day found me with my 'vis-a-vis' and four at the door of Donna Cecilia, who came with me as before. The charming widow, notwithstanding her strict morality, was delighted at my love for her daughter. The family rode in a large phaeton hired by Don Francisco, which gave room for six persons.

At half-past seven in the morning we made a halt at a small place where had been prepared, by Don Franciso's orders, an excellent breakfast, which was intended to replace the dinner, and we all made a hearty meal, as we were not likely to find time for anything but supper at Tivoli. I wore on my finger the beautiful ring which Lucrezia had given me. At the back of the ring I had had a piece of enamel placed, on it was delineated a saduceus, with one serpent between the letters Alpha and Omega. This ring was the subject of conversation during breakfast, and Don Francisco, as well as the advocate, exerted himself in vain to guess the meaning of the hieroglyphs; much to the amusement of Lucrezia, who understood the mysterious secret so well. We continued our road, and reached Tivoli at ten o'clock.

We began by visiting Don Francisco's villa. It was a beautiful little house, and we spent the following six hours in examining together the antiquities of Tivoli. Lucrezia having occasion to whisper a few words to Don Francisco, I seized the opportunity of telling Angelique that after her marriage I should be happy to spend a few days of the fine season with her.

"Sir," she answered, "I give you fair notice that the moment I become mistress in this house you will be the very first person to be excluded."

"I feel greatly obliged to you, signora, for your timely notice."

But the most amusing part of the affair was that I construed Angelique's wanton insult into a declaration of love. I was astounded. Lucrezia, remarking the state I was in, touched my arm, enquiring what ailed me. I told her, and she said at once,

"My darling, my happiness cannot last long; the cruel moment of our separation is drawing near. When I have gone, pray undertake the task of compelling her to acknowledge her error. Angelique pities me, be sure to avenge me."

I have forgotten to mention that at Don Francisco's villa I happened to praise a very pretty room opening upon the orange-house, and the amiable host, having heard me, came obligingly to me, and said that it should be my room that night. Lucrezia feigned not to hear, but it was to her Ariadne's clue, for, as we were to remain altogether during our visit to the beauties of Tivoli, we had no chance of a tete-a-tete through the day.

I have said that we devoted six hours to an examination of the antiquities of Tivoli, but I am bound to confess here that I saw, for my part, very little of them, and it was only twenty-eight years later that I made a thorough acquaintance with the beautiful spot.

We returned to the villa towards evening, fatigued and very hungry, but an hour's rest before supper—a repast which lasted two hours, the most delicious dishes, the most exquisite wines, and particularly the excellent wine of Tivoli—restored us so well that everybody wanted nothing more than a good bed and the freedom to enjoy the bed according to his own taste.

As everybody objected to sleep alone, Lucrezia said that she would sleep with Angelique in one of the rooms leading to the orange-house, and proposed that her husband should share a room with the young abbe, his brother-in-law, and that Donna Cecilia should take her youngest daughter with her.

The arrangement met with general approbation, and Don Francisco, taking a candle, escorted me to my pretty little room adjoining the one in which the two sisters were to sleep, and, after shewing me how I could lock myself in, he wished me good night and left me alone.

Angelique had no idea that I was her near neighbour, but Lucrezia and I, without exchanging a single word on the subject, had perfectly understood each other.

I watched through the key-hole and saw the two sisters come into their room, preceded by the polite Don Francisco, who carried a taper, and, after lighting a night-lamp, bade them good night and retired. Then my two beauties, their door once locked, sat down on the sofa and completed their night toilet, which, in that fortunate climate, is similar to the costume of our first mother. Lucrezia, knowing that I was waiting to come in, told her sister to lie down on the side towards the window, and the virgin, having no idea that she was exposing her most secret beauties to my profane eyes, crossed the room in a state of complete nakedness. Lucrezia put out the lamp and lay down near her innocent sister.

Happy moments which I can no longer enjoy, but the sweet remembrance of which death alone can make me lose! I believe I never undressed myself as quickly as I did that evening.

I open the door and fall into the arms of my Lucrezia, who says to her sister, "It is my angel, my love; never mind him, and go to sleep."

What a delightful picture I could offer to my readers if it were possible for me to paint voluptuousnes in its most enchanting colours!

What ecstasies of love from the very onset! What delicious raptures succeed each other until the sweetest fatigue made us give way to the soothing influence of Morpheus!

The first rays of the sun, piercing through the crevices of the shutters, wake us out of our refreshing slumbers, and like two valorous knights who have ceased fighting only to renew the contest with increased ardour, we lose no time in giving ourselves up to all the intensity of the flame which consumes us.

"Oh, my beloved Lucrezia! how supremely happy I am! But, my darling, mind your sister; she might turn round and see us."

"Fear nothing, my life; my sister is kind, she loves me, she pities me; do you not love me, my dear Angelique? Oh! turn round, see how happy your sister is, and know what felicity awaits you when you own the sway of love."

Angelique, a young maiden of seventeen summers, who must have suffered the torments of Tantalus during the night, and who only wishes for a pretext to shew that she has forgiven her sister, turns round, and covering her sister with kisses, confesses that she has not closed her eyes through the night.

"Then forgive likewise, darling Angelique, forgive him who loves me, and whom I adore," says Lucrezia.

Unfathomable power of the god who conquers all human beings!

"Angelique hates me," I say, "I dare not. . ."

"No, I do not hate you!" answers the charming girl.

"Kiss her, dearest," says Lucrezia, pushing me towards her sister, and pleased to see her in my arms motionless and languid.

But sentiment, still more than love, forbids me to deprive Lucrezia of the proof of my gratitude, and I turn to her with all the rapture of a beginner, feeling that my ardour is increased by Angelique's ecstasy, as for the first time she witnesses the amorous contest. Lucrezia, dying of enjoyment, entreats me to stop, but, as I do not listen to her prayer, she tricks me, and the sweet Angelique makes her first sacrifice to the mother of love. It is thus, very likely, that when the gods inhabited this earth, the voluptuous Arcadia, in love with the soft and pleasing breath of Zephyrus, one day opened her arms, and was fecundated.

Lucrezia was astonished and delighted, and covered us both with kisses. Angelique, as happy as her sister, expired deliciously in my arms for the third time, and she seconded me with so much loving ardour, that it seemed to me I was tasting happiness for the first time.

Phoebus had left the nuptial couch, and his rays were already diffusing light over the universe; and that light, reaching us through the closed shutters, gave me warning to quit the place; we exchanged the most loving adieus, I left my two divinities and retired to my own room. A few minutes afterwards, the cheerful voice of the advocate was heard in the chamber of the sisters; he was reproaching them for sleeping too long! Then he knocked at my door, threatening to bring the ladies to me, and went away, saying that he would send me the hair-dresser.

After many ablutions and a careful toilet, I thought I could skew my face, and I presented myself coolly in the drawing-room. The two sisters were there with the other members of our society, and I was delighted with their rosy cheeks. Lucrezia was frank and gay, and beamed with happiness; Angelique, as fresh as the morning dew, was more radiant than usual, but fidgety, and carefully avoided looking me in the face. I saw that my useless attempts to catch her eyes made her smile, and I remarked to her mother, rather mischievously, that it was a pity Angelique used paint for her face. She was duped by this stratagem, and compelled me to pass a handkerchief over her face, and was then obliged to look at me. I offered her my apologies, and Don Francisco appeared highly pleased that the complexion of his intended had met with such triumph.

After breakfast we took a walk through the garden, and, finding myself alone with Lucrezia, I expostulated tenderly with her for having almost thrown her sister in my arms.

"Do not reproach me," she said, "when I deserve praise. I have brought light into the darkness of my charming sister's soul; I have initiated her in the sweetest of mysteries, and now, instead of pitying me, she must envy me. Far from having hatred for you, she must love you dearly, and as I am so unhappy as to have to part from you very soon, my beloved, I leave her to you; she will replace me."

"Ah, Lucrezia! how can I love her?"

"Is she not a charming girl?"

"No doubt of it; but my adoration for you is a shield against any other love. Besides Don Francisco must, of course, entirely monopolize her, and I do not wish to cause coolness between them, or to ruin the peace of their home. I am certain your sister is not like you, and I would bet that, even now, she upbraids herself for having given way to the ardour of her temperament:"

"Most likely; but, dearest, I am sorry to say my husband expects to obtain judgment in the course of this week, and then the short instants of happiness will for ever be lost to me."

This was sad news indeed, and to cause a diversion at the breakfast-table I took much notice of the generous Don Francisco, and promised to compose a nuptial song for his wedding-day, which had been fixed for the early part of January.

We returned to Rome, and for the three hours that she was with me in my vis-a-vis, Lucrezia had no reason to think that my ardour was at all abated. But when we reached the city I was rather fatigued, and proceeded at once to the palace.

Lucrezia had guessed rightly; her husband obtained his judgment three or four days afterwards, and called upon me to announce their departure for the day after the morrow; he expressed his warm friendship for me, and by his invitation I spent the two last evenings with Lucrezia, but we were always surrounded by the family. The day of her departure, wishing to cause her an agreeable surprise, I left Rome before them and waited for them at the place where I thought they would put up for the night, but the advocate, having been detained by several engagements, was detained in Rome, and they only reached the place next day for dinner. We dined together, we exchanged a sad, painful farewell, and they continued their journey while I returned to Rome.

After the departure of this charming woman, I found myself in sort of solitude very natural to a young man whose heart is not full of hope.

I passed whole days in my room, making extracts from the French letters written by the cardinal, and his eminence was kind enough to tell me that my extracts were judiciously made, but that he insisted upon my not working so hard. The beautiful marchioness was present when he paid me that compliment.

Since my second visit to her, I had not presented myself at her house; she was consequently rather cool to me, and, glad of an opportunity of making me feel her displeasure, she remarked to his eminence that very likely work was a consolation to me in the great void caused by the departure of Donna Lucrezia.

"I candidly confess, madam, that I have felt her loss deeply. She was kind and generous; above all, she was indulgent when I did not call often upon her. My friendship for her was innocent."

"I have no doubt of it, although your ode was the work of a poet deeply in love."

"Oh!" said the kindly cardinal, "a poet cannot possibly write without professing to be in love."

"But," replied the marchioness, "if the poet is really in love, he has no need of professing a feeling which he possesses."

As she was speaking, the marchioness drew out of her pocket a paper which she offered to his eminence.

"This is the ode," she said, "it does great honour to the poet, for it is admitted to be a masterpiece by all the literati in Rome, and Donna Lucrezia knows it by heart."

The cardinal read it over and returned it, smiling, and remarking that, as he had no taste for Italian poetry, she must give herself the pleasure of translating it into French rhyme if she wished him to admire it.

"I only write French prose," answered the marchioness, "and a prose translation destroys half the beauty of poetry. I am satisfied with writing occasionally a little Italian poetry without any pretension to poetical fame."

Those words were accompanied by a very significant glance in my direction.

"I should consider myself fortunate, madam, if I could obtain the happiness of admiring some of your poetry."

"Here is a sonnet of her ladyship's," said Cardinal S. C.

I took it respectfully, and I prepared to read it, but the amiable marchioness told me to put it in my pocket and return it to the cardinal the next day, although she did not think the sonnet worth so much trouble. "If you should happen to go out in the morning," said Cardinal S. C., "you could bring it back, and dine with me." Cardinal Aquaviva immediately answered for me: "He will be sure to go out purposely."

With a deep reverence, which expressed my thanks, I left the room quietly and returned to my apartment, very impatient to read the sonnet. Yet, before satisfying my wish, I could not help making some reflections on the situation. I began to think myself somebody since the gigantic stride I had made this evening at the cardinal's assembly. The Marchioness de G. had shewn in the most open way the interest she felt in me, and, under cover of her grandeur, had not hesitated to compromise herself publicly by the most flattering advances. But who would have thought of disapproving? A young abbe like me, without any importance whatever, who could scarcely pretend to her high protection! True, but she was precisely the woman to grant it to those who, feeling themselves unworthy of it, dared not shew any pretensions to her patronage. On that head, my modesty must be evident to everyone, and the marchioness would certainly have insulted me had she supposed me capable of sufficient vanity to fancy that she felt the slightest inclination for me. No, such a piece of self-conceit was not in accordance with my nature. Her cardinal himself had invited me to dinner. Would he have done so if he had admitted the possibility of the beautiful marchioness feeling anything for me? Of course not, and he gave me an invitation to dine with him only because he had understood, from the very words of the lady, that I was just the sort of person with whom they could converse for a few hours without any risk; to be sure, without any risk whatever. Oh, Master Casanova! do you really think so?

Well, why should I put on a mask before my readers? They may think me conceited if they please, but the fact of the matter is that I felt sure of having made a conquest of the marchioness. I congratulated myself because she had taken the first, most difficult, and most important step. Had she not done so, I should never have dared-to lay siege to her even in the most approved fashion; I should never have even ventured to dream of winning her. It was only this evening that I thought she might replace Lucrezia. She was beautiful, young, full of wit and talent; she was fond of literary pursuits, and very powerful in Rome; what more was necessary? Yet I thought it would be good policy to appear ignorant of her inclination for me, and to let her suppose from the very next day that I was in love with her, but that my love appeared to me hopeless. I knew that such a plan was infallible, because it saved her dignity. It seemed to me that Father Georgi himself would be compelled to approve such an undertaking, and I had remarked with great satisfaction that Cardinal Acquaviva had expressed his delight at Cardinal S. C.'s invitation—an honour which he had never yet bestowed on me himself. This affair might have very important results for me.

I read the marchioness's sonnet, and found it easy, flowing, and well written. It was composed in praise of the King of Prussia, who had just conquered Silesia by a masterly stroke. As I was copying it, the idea struck me to personify Silesia, and to make her, in answer to the sonnet, bewail that Love (supposed to be the author of the sonnet of the marchioness) could applaud the man who had conquered her, when that conqueror was the sworn enemy of Love.

It is impossible for a man accustomed to write poetry to abstain when a happy subject smiles upon his delighted imagination. If he attempted to smother the poetical flame running through his veins it would consume him. I composed my sonnet, keeping the same rhymes as in the original, and, well pleased with my muse, I went to bed.

The next morning the Abbe Gama came in just as I had finished recopying my sonnet, and said he would breakfast with me. He complimented me upon the honour conferred on me by the invitation of Cardinal S. C.

"But be prudent," he added, "for his eminence has the reputation of being jealous."

I thanked him for his friendly advice, taking care to assure him that I had nothing to fear, because I did not feel the slightest inclination for the handsome marchioness.

Cardinal S. C. received me with great kindness mingled with dignity, to make me realize the importance of the favour he was bestowing upon me.

"What do you think," he enquired, "of the sonnet?"

"Monsignor, it is perfectly written, and, what is more, it is a charming composition. Allow me to return it to you with my thanks."

"She has much talent. I wish to shew you ten stanzas of her composition, my dear abbe, but you must promise to be very discreet about it."

"Your eminence may rely on me."

He opened his bureau and brought forth the stanzas of which he was the subject. I read them, found them well written, but devoid of enthusiasm; they were the work of a poet, and expressed love in the words of passion, but were not pervaded by that peculiar feeling by which true love is so easily discovered. The worthy cardinal was doubtless guilty of a very great indiscretion, but self-love is the cause of so many injudicious steps! I asked his eminence whether he had answered the stanzas.

"No," he replied, "I have not; but would you feel disposed to lend me your poetical pen, always under the seal of secrecy?"

"As to secrecy, monsignor, I promise it faithfully; but I am afraid the marchioness will remark the difference between your style and mine."

"She has nothing of my composition," said the cardinal; "I do not think she supposes me a fine poet, and for that reason your stanzas must be written in such a manner that she will not esteem them above my abilities."

"I will write them with pleasure, monsignor, and your eminence can form an opinion; if they do not seem good enough to be worthy of you, they need not be given to the marchioness."

"That is well said. Will you write them at once?"

"What! now, monsignor? It is not like prose."

"Well, well! try to let me have them to-morrow."

We dined alone, and his eminence complimented me upon my excellent appetite, which he remarked was as good as his own; but I was beginning to understand my eccentric host, and, to flatter him, I answered that he praised me more than I deserved, and that my appetite was inferior to his. The singular compliment delighted him, and I saw all the use I could make of his eminence.

Towards the end of the dinner, as we were conversing, the marchioness made her appearance, and, as a matter of course, without being announced. Her looks threw me into raptures; I thought her a perfect beauty. She did not give the cardinal time to meet her, but sat down near him, while I remained standing, according to etiquette.

Without appearing to notice me, the marchioness ran wittily over various topics until coffee was brought in. Then, addressing herself to me, she told me to sit down, just as if she was bestowing charity upon me.

"By-the-by, abbe," she said, a minute after, "have you read my sonnet?"

"Yes, madam, and I have had the honour to return it to his eminence. I have found it so perfect that I am certain it must have cost you a great deal of time."

"Time?" exclaimed the cardinal; "Oh! you do not know the marchioness."

"Monsignor," I replied, "nothing can be done well without time, and that is why I have not dared to chew to your eminence an answer to the sonnet which I have written in half an hour."

"Let us see it, abbe," said the marchioness; "I want to read it."

"Answer of Silesia to Love." This title brought the most fascinating blushes on her countenance. "But Love is not mentioned in the sonnet," exclaimed the cardinal. "Wait," said the marchioness, "we must respect the idea of the poet:"

She read the sonnet over and over, and thought that the reproaches addressed by Silesia to Love were very just. She explained my idea to the cardinal, making him understand why Silesia was offended at having been conquered by the King of Prussia.

"Ah, I see, I see!" exclaimed the cardinal, full of joy; "Silesia is a woman. . . and the King of Prussia. . . Oh! oh! that is really a fine idea!" And the good cardinal laughed heartily for more than a quarter of an hour. "I must copy that sonnet," he added, "indeed I must have it."

"The abbe," said the obliging marchioness, "will save you the trouble: I will dictate it to him."

I prepared to write, but his eminence suddenly exclaimed, "My dear marchioness, this is wonderful; he has kept the same rhymes as in your own sonnet: did you observe it?"

The beautiful marchioness gave me then a look of such expression that she completed her conquest. I understood that she wanted me to know the cardinal as well as she knew him; it was a kind of partnership in which I was quite ready to play my part.

As soon as I had written the sonnet under the charming woman's dictation, I took my leave, but not before the cardinal had told me that he expected me to dinner the next day.

I had plenty of work before me, for the ten stanzas I had to compose were of the most singular character, and I lost no time in shutting myself up in my room to think of them. I had to keep my balance between two points of equal difficulty, and I felt that great care was indispensable. I had to place the marchioness in such a position that she could pretend to believe the cardinal the author of the stanzas, and, at the same time, compel her to find out that I had written them, and that I was aware of her knowing it. It was necessary to speak so carefully that not one expression should breathe even the faintest hope on my part, and yet to make my stanzas blaze with the ardent fire of my love under the thin veil of poetry. As for the cardinal, I knew well enough that the better the stanzas were written, the more disposed he would be to sign them. All I wanted was clearness, so difficult to obtain in poetry, while a little doubtful darkness would have been accounted sublime by my new Midas. But, although I wanted to please him, the cardinal was only a secondary consideration, and the handsome marchioness the principal object.

As the marchioness in her verses had made a pompous enumeration of every physical and moral quality of his eminence, it was of course natural that he should return the compliment, and here my task was easy. At last having mastered my subject well, I began my work, and giving full career to my imagination and to my feelings I composed the ten stanzas, and gave the finishing stroke with these two beautiful lines from Ariosto:

Le angelicche bellezze nate al cielo
Non si ponno celar sotto alcum velo.

Rather pleased with my production, I presented it the next day to the cardinal, modestly saying that I doubted whether he would accept the authorship of so ordinary a composition. He read the stanzas twice over without taste or expression, and said at last that they were indeed not much, but exactly what he wanted. He thanked me particularly for the two lines from Ariosto, saying that they would assist in throwing the authorship upon himself, as they would prove to the lady for whom they were intended that he had not been able to write them without borrowing. And, as to offer me some consolation, he told me that, in recopying the lines, he would take care to make a few mistakes in the rhythm to complete the illusion.

We dined earlier than the day before, and I withdrew immediately after dinner so as to give him leisure to make a copy of the stanzas before the arrival of the lady.

The next evening I met the marchioness at the entrance of the palace, and offered her my arm to come out of her carriage. The instant she alighted, she said to me,

"If ever your stanzas and mine become known in Rome, you may be sure of my enmity."

"Madam, I do not understand what you mean."

"I expected you to answer me in this manner," replied the marchioness, "but recollect what I have said."

I left her at the door of the reception-room, and thinking that she was really angry with me, I went away in despair. "My stanzas," I said to myself, "are too fiery; they compromise her dignity, and her pride is offended at my knowing the secret of her intrigue with Cardinal S. C. Yet, I feel certain that the dread she expresses of my want of discretion is only feigned, it is but a pretext to turn me out of her favour. She has not understood my reserve! What would she have done, if I had painted her in the simple apparel of the golden age, without any of those veils which modesty imposes upon her sex!" I was sorry I had not done so. I undressed and went to bed. My head was scarcely on the pillow when the Abbe Gama knocked at my door. I pulled the door-string, and coming in, he said,

"My dear sir, the cardinal wishes to see you, and I am sent by the beautiful marchioness and Cardinal S. C., who desire you to come down."

"I am very sorry, but I cannot go; tell them the truth; I am ill in bed."

As the abbe did not return, I judged that he had faithfully acquitted himself of the commission, and I spent a quiet night. I was not yet dressed in the morning, when I received a note from Cardinal S. C. inviting me to dinner, saying that he had just been bled, and that he wanted to speak to me: he concluded by entreating me to come to him early, even if I did not feel well.

The invitation was pressing; I could not guess what had caused it, but the tone of the letter did not forebode anything unpleasant. I went to church, where I was sure that Cardinal Acquaviva would see me, and he did. After mass, his eminence beckoned to me.

"Are you truly ill?" he enquired.

"No, monsignor, I was only sleepy."

"I am very glad to hear it; but you are wrong, for you are loved. Cardinal S. C. has been bled this morning."

"I know it, monsignor. The cardinal tells me so in this note, in which he invites me to dine with him, with your excellency's permission."

"Certainly. But this is amusing! I did not know that he wanted a third person."

"Will there be a third person?"

"I do not know, and I have no curiosity about it."

The cardinal left me, and everybody imagined that his eminence had spoken to me of state affairs.

I went to my new Maecenas, whom I found in bed.

"I am compelled to observe strict diet," he said to me; "I shall have to let you dine alone, but you will not lose by it as my cook does not know it. What I wanted to tell you is that your stanzas are, I am afraid, too pretty, for the marchioness adores them. If you had read them to me in the same way that she does, I could never have made up my mind to offer them." "But she believes them to be written by your eminence?"

"Of course."

"That is the essential point, monsignor."

"Yes; but what should I do if she took it into her head to compose some new stanzas for me?"

"You would answer through the same pen, for you can dispose of me night and day, and rely upon the utmost secrecy."

"I beg of you to accept this small present; it is some negrillo snuff from Habana, which Cardinal Acquaviva has given me."

The snuff was excellent, but the object which contained it was still better. It was a splendid gold-enamelled box. I received it with respect, and with the expression of the deepest gratitude.

If his eminence did not know how to write poetry, at least he knew how to be generous, and in a delicate manner, and that science is, at least in my estimation, superior to the other for a great nobleman.

At noon, and much to my surprise, the beautiful marchioness made her appearance in the most elegant morning toilet.

"If I had known you were in good company," she said to the cardinal, "I would not have come."

"I am sure, dear marchioness, you will not find our dear abbe in the way."

"No, for I believe him to be honest and true."

I kept at a respectful distance, ready to go away with my splendid snuff-box at the first jest she might hurl at me.

The cardinal asked her if she intended to remain to dinner.

"Yes," she answered; "but I shall not enjoy my dinner, for I hate to eat alone."

"If you would honour him so far, the abbe would keep you company."

She gave me a gracious look, but without uttering one word.

This was the first time I had anything to do with a woman of quality, and that air of patronage, whatever kindness might accompany it, always put me out of temper, for I thought it made love out of the question. However, as we were in the presence of the cardinal, I fancied that she might be right in treating me in that fashion.

The table was laid out near the cardinal's bed, and the marchioness, who ate hardly anything, encouraged me in my good appetite.

"I have told you that the abbe is equal to me in that respect," said S. C.

"I truly believe," answered the marchioness, "that he does not remain far behind you; but," added she with flattery, "you are more dainty in your tastes."

"Would her ladyship be so good as to tell me in what I have appeared to her to be a mere glutton? For in all things I like only dainty and exquisite morsels."

"Explain what you mean by saying in all things," said the cardinal. Taking the liberty of laughing, I composed a few impromptu verses in which I named all I thought dainty and exquisite. The marchioness applauded, saying that she admired my courage.

"My courage, madam, is due to you, for I am as timid as a hare when I am not encouraged; you are the author of my impromptu."

"I admire you. As for myself, were I encouraged by Apollo himself, I could not compose four lines without paper and ink."

"Only give way boldly to your genius, madam, and you will produce poetry worthy of heaven."

"That—is my opinion, too," said the cardinal. "I entreat you to give me permission to skew your ten stanzas to the abbe."

"They are not very good, but I have no objection provided it remains between us."

The cardinal gave me, then, the stanzas composed by the marchioness, and I read them aloud with all the expression, all the feeling necessary to such reading.

"How well you have read those stanzas!" said the marchioness; "I can hardly believe them to be my own composition; I thank you very much. But have the goodness to give the benefit of your reading to the stanzas which his eminence has written in answer to mine. They surpass them much."

"Do not believe it, my dear abbe," said the cardinal, handing them to me. "Yet try not to let them lose anything through your reading."

There was certainly no need of his eminence enforcing upon me such a recommendation; it was my own poetry. I could not have read it otherwise than in my best style, especially when I had before me the beautiful woman who had inspired them, and when, besides, Bacchus was in me giving courage to Apollo as much as the beautiful eyes of the marchioness were fanning into an ardent blaze the fire already burning through my whole being.

I read the stanzas with so much expression that the cardinal was enraptured, but I brought a deep carnation tint upon the cheeks of the lovely marchioness when I came to the description of those beauties which the imagination of the poet is allowed to guess at, but which I could not, of course, have gazed upon. She snatched the paper from my hands with passion, saying that I was adding verses of my own; it was true, but I did not confess it. I was all aflame, and the fire was scorching her as well as me.

The cardinal having fallen asleep, she rose and went to take a seat on the balcony; I followed her. She had a rather high seat; I stood opposite to her, so that her knee touched the fob-pocket in which was my watch. What a position! Taking hold gently of one of her hands,

I told her that she had ignited in my soul a devouring flame, that I adored her, and that, unless some hope was left to me of finding her sensible to my sufferings, I was determined to fly away from her for ever.

"Yes, beautiful marchioness, pronounce my sentence."

"I fear you are a libertine and an unfaithful lover."

"I am neither one nor the other."

With these words I folded her in my arms, and I pressed upon her lovely lips, as pure as a rose, an ardent kiss which she received with the best possible grace. This kiss, the forerunner of the most delicious pleasures, had imparted to my hands the greatest boldness; I was on the point of. . . but the marchioness, changing her position, entreated me so sweetly to respect her, that, enjoying new voluptuousness through my very obedience, I not only abandoned an easy victory, but I even begged her pardon, which I soon read in the most loving look.

She spoke of Lucrezia, and was pleased with my discretion. She then alluded to the cardinal, doing her best to make me believe that there was nothing between them but a feeling of innocent friendship. Of course I had my opinion on that subject, but it was my interest to appear to believe every word she uttered. We recited together lines from our best poets, and all the time she was still sitting down and I standing before her, with my looks rapt in the contemplation of the most lovely charms, to which I remained insensible in appearance, for I had made up my mind not to press her that evening for greater favours than those I had already received.

The cardinal, waking from his long and peaceful siesta, got up and joined us in his night-cap, and good-naturedly enquired whether we had not felt impatient at his protracted sleep. I remained until dark and went home highly pleased with my day's work, but determined to keep my ardent desires in check until the opportunity for complete victory offered itself.

From that day, the charming marchioness never ceased to give me the marks of her particular esteem, without the slightest constraint; I was reckoning upon the carnival, which was close at hand, feeling certain that the more I should spare her delicacy, the more she would endeavour to find the opportunity of rewarding my loyalty, and of crowning with happiness my loving constancy. But fate ordained otherwise; Dame Fortune turned her back upon me at the very moment when the Pope and Cardinal Acquaviva were thinking of giving me a really good position.

The Holy Father had congratulated me upon the beautiful snuff-box presented to me by Cardinal S. C., but he had been careful never to name the marchioness. Cardinal Acquaviva expressed openly his delight at his brother-cardinal having given me a taste of his negrillo snuff in so splendid an envelope; the Abbe Gama, finding me so forward on the road to success, did not venture to counsel me any more, and the virtuous Father Georgi gave me but one piece of advice-namely, to cling to the lovely marchioness and not to make any other acquaintances.

Such was my position-truly a brilliant one, when, on Christmas Day, the lover of Barbara Dalacqua entered my room, locked the door, and threw himself on the sofa, exclaiming that I saw him for the last time.

"I only come to beg of you some good advice."

"On what subject can I advise you?"

"Take this and read it; it will explain everything."

It was a letter from his mistress; the contents were these:

"I am pregnant of a child, the pledge of our mutual love; I can no longer have any doubt of it, my beloved, and I forewarn you that I have made up my mind to quit Rome alone, and to go away to die where it may please God, if you refuse to take care of me and save me. I would suffer anything, do anything, rather than let my father discover the truth."

"If you are a man of honour," I said, "you cannot abandon the poor girl. Marry her in spite of your father, in spite of her own, and live together honestly. The eternal Providence of God will watch over you and help you in your difficulties:"

My advice seemed to bring calm to his mind, and he left me more composed.

At the beginning of January, 1744, he called again, looking very cheerful. "I have hired," he said, "the top floor of the house next to Barbara's dwelling; she knows it, and to-night I will gain her apartment through one of the windows of the garret, and we will make all our arrangements to enable me to carry her off. I have made up my mind; I have decided upon taking her to Naples, and I will take with us the servant who, sleeping in the garret, had to be made a confidante of."

"God speed you, my friend!"

A week afterwards, towards eleven o'clock at night, he entered my room accompanied by an abbe.

"What do you want so late?"

"I wish to introduce you to this handsome abbe."

I looked up, and to my consternation I recognized Barbara.

"Has anyone seen you enter the house?" I enquired.

"No; and if we had been seen, what of it? It is only an abbe. We now pass every night together."

"I congratulate you."

"The servant is our friend; she has consented to follow us, and all our arrangements are completed."

"I wish you every happiness. Adieu. I beg you to leave me."

Three or four days after that visit, as I was walking with the Abbe Gama towards the Villa Medicis, he told me deliberately that there would be an execution during the night in the Piazza di Spagna.

"What kind of execution?"

"The bargello or his lieutenant will come to execute some 'ordine santissimo', or to visit some suspicious dwelling in order to arrest and carry off some person who does not expect anything of the sort."

"How do you know it?"

"His eminence has to know it, for the Pope would not venture to encroach upon his jurisdiction without asking his permission."

"And his eminence has given it?"

"Yes, one of the Holy Father's auditors came for that purpose this morning."

"But the cardinal might have refused?"

"Of course; but such a permission is never denied."

"And if the person to be arrested happened to be under the protection of the cardinal—what then?"

"His eminence would give timely warning to that person."

We changed the conversation, but the news had disturbed me. I fancied that the execution threatened Barbara and her lover, for her father's house was under the Spanish jurisdiction. I tried to see the young man but I could not succeed in meeting him, and I was afraid lest a visit at his home or at M. Dalacqua's dwelling might implicate me. Yet it is certain that this last consideration would not have stopped me if I had been positively sure that they were threatened; had I felt satisfied of their danger, I would have braved everything.

About midnight, as I was ready to go to bed, and just as I was opening my door to take the key from outside, an abbe rushed panting into my room and threw himself on a chair. It was Barbara; I guessed what had taken place, and, foreseeing all the evil consequences her visit might have for me, deeply annoyed and very anxious, I upbraided her for having taken refuge in my room, and entreated her to go away.

Fool that I was! Knowing that I was only ruining myself without any chance of saving her, I ought to have compelled her to leave my room, I ought to have called for the servants if she had refused to withdraw. But I had not courage enough, or rather I voluntarily obeyed the decrees of destiny.

When she heard my order to go away, she threw herself on her knees, and melting into tears, she begged, she entreated my pity!

Where is the heart of steel which is not softened by the tears, by the prayers of a pretty and unfortunate woman? I gave way, but I told her that it was ruin for both of us.

"No one," she replied, "has seen me, I am certain, when I entered the mansion and came up to your room, and I consider my visit here a week ago as most fortunate; otherwise, I never could have known which was your room."

"Alas! how much better if you had never come! But what has become of your lover?"

"The 'sbirri' have carried him off, as well as the servant. I will tell you all about it. My lover had informed me that a carriage would wait to-night at the foot of the flight of steps before the Church of Trinita del Monte, and that he would be there himself. I entered his room through the garret window an hour ago. There I put on this disguise, and, accompanied by the servant, proceeded to meet him. The servant walked a few yards before me, and carried a parcel of my things. At the corner of the street, one of the buckles of my shoes being unfastened, I stopped an instant, and the servant went on, thinking that I was following her. She reached the carriage, got into it, and, as I was getting nearer, the light from a lantern disclosed to me some thirty sbirri; at the same instant, one of them got on the driver's box and drove off at full speed, carrying off the servant, whom they must have mistaken for me, and my lover who was in the coach awaiting me. What could I do at such a fearful moment? I could not go back to my father's house, and I followed my first impulse which brought me here. And here I am! You tell me that my presence will cause your ruin; if it is so, tell me what to do; I feel I am dying; but find some expedient and I am ready to do anything, even to lay my life down, rather than be the cause of your ruin."

But she wept more bitterly than ever.

Her position was so sad that I thought it worse even than mine, although I could almost fancy I saw ruin before me despite my innocence.

"Let me," I said, "conduct you to your father; I feel sure of obtaining your pardon."

But my proposal only enhanced her fears.

"I am lost," she exclaimed; "I know my father. Ah! reverend sir, turn me out into the street, and abandon me to my miserable fate."

No doubt I ought to have done so, and I would have done it if the consciousness of what was due to my own interest had been stronger than my feeling of pity. But her tears! I have often said it, and those amongst my readers who have experienced it, must be of the same opinion; there is nothing on earth more irresistible than two beautiful eyes shedding tears, when the owner of those eyes is handsome, honest, and unhappy. I found myself physically unable to send her away.

"My poor girl," I said at last, "when daylight comes, and that will not be long, for it is past midnight, what do you intend to do?"

"I must leave the palace," she replied, sobbing. "In this disguise no one can recognize me; I will leave Rome, and I will walk straight before me until I fall on the ground, dying with grief and fatigue."

With these words she fell on the floor. She was choking; I could see her face turn blue; I was in the greatest distress.

I took off her neck-band, unlaced her stays under the abbe's dress, I threw cold water in her face, and I finally succeeded in bringing her back to consciousness.

The night was extremely cold, and there was no fire in my room. I advised her to get into my bed, promising to respect her.

"Alas! reverend sir, pity is the only feeling with which I can now inspire anyone."

And, to speak the truth I was too deeply moved, and, at the same time, too full of anxiety, to leave room in me for any desire. Having induced her to go to bed, and her extreme weakness preventing her from doing anything for herself, I undressed her and put her to bed, thus proving once more that compassion will silence the most imperious requirements of nature, in spite of all the charms which would, under other circumstances, excite to the highest degree the senses of a man. I lay down near her in my clothes, and woke her at day-break. Her strength was somewhat restored, she dressed herself alone, and I left my room, telling her to keep quiet until my return. I intended to proceed to her father's house, and to solicit her pardon, but, having perceived some suspicious-looking men loitering about the palace, I thought it wise to alter my mind, and went to a coffeehouse.

I soon ascertained that a spy was watching my movements at a distance; but I did not appear to notice him, and having taken some chocolate and stored a few biscuits in my pocket, I returned towards the palace, apparently without any anxiety or hurry, always followed by the same individual. I judged that the bargello, having failed in his project, was now reduced to guesswork, and I was strengthened in that view of the case when the gate-keeper of the palace told, without my asking any question, as I came in, that an arrest had been attempted during the night, and had not succeeded. While he was speaking, one of the auditors of the Vicar-General called to enquire when he could see the Abby Gama. I saw that no time was to be lost, and went up to my room to decide upon what was to be done.

I began by making the poor girl eat a couple of biscuits soaked in some Canary wine, and I took her afterwards to the top story of the palace, where, leaving her in a not very decent closet which was not used by anyone, I told her to wait for me.

My servant came soon after, and I ordered him to lock the door of my room as soon as he finished cleaning it, and to bring me the key at the Abbe Gama's apartment, where I was going. I found Gama in conversation with the auditor sent by the Vicar-General. As soon as he had dismissed him, he came to me, and ordered his servant to serve the chocolate. When we were left alone he gave me an account of his interview with the auditor, who had come to entreat his eminence to give orders to turn out of his palace a person who was supposed to have taken refuge in it about midnight. "We must wait," said the abbe, "until the cardinal is visible, but I am quite certain that, if anyone has taken refuge here unknown to him, his eminence will compel that person to leave the palace." We then spoke of the weather and other trifles until my servant brought my key. Judging that I had at least an hour to spare, I bethought myself of a plan which alone could save Barbara from shame and misery.

Feeling certain that I was unobserved, I went up to my poor prisoner and made her write the following words in French:

"I am an honest girl, monsignor, though I am disguised in the dress of an abbe. I entreat your eminence to allow me to give my name only to you and in person. I hope that, prompted by the great goodness of your soul, your eminence will save me from dishonour." I gave her the necessary instructions, as to sending the note to the cardinal, assuring her that he would have her brought to him as soon as he read it.

"When you are in his presence," I added, "throw yourself on your knees, tell him everything without any concealment, except as regards your having passed the night in my room. You must be sure not to mention that circumstance, for the cardinal must remain in complete ignorance of my knowing anything whatever of this intrigue. Tell him that, seeing your lover carried off, you rushed to his palace and ran upstairs as far as you could go, and that after a most painful night Heaven inspired you with the idea of writing to him to entreat his pity. I feel certain that, one way or the other, his eminence will save you from dishonour, and it certainly is the only chance you have of being united to the man you love so dearly."

She promised to follow 'my instructions faithfully, and, coming down, I had my hair dressed and went to church, where the cardinal saw me. I then went out and returned only for dinner, during which the only subject of conversation was the adventure of the night. Gama alone said nothing, and I followed his example, but I understood from all the talk going on round the table that the cardinal had taken my poor Barbara under his protection. That was all I wanted, and thinking that I had nothing more to fear I congratulated myself, in petto, upon my stratagem, which had, I thought, proved a master-stroke. After dinner, finding myself alone with Gama, I asked him what was the meaning of it all, and this is what he told me:

"A father, whose name I do not know yet, had requested the assistance of the Vicar-General to prevent his son from carrying off a young girl, with whom he intended to leave the States of the Church; the pair had arranged to meet at midnight in this very square, and the Vicar, having previously obtained the consent of our cardinal, as I told you yesterday, gave orders to the bargello to dispose his men in such a way as to catch the young people in the very act of running away, and to arrest them. The orders were executed, but the 'sbirri' found out, when they returned to the bargello, that they had met with only a half success, the woman who got out of the carriage with the young man not belonging to that species likely to be carried off. Soon afterwards a spy informed the bargello that, at the very moment the arrest was executed, he had seen a young abbe run away very rapidly and take refuge in this palace, and the suspicion immediately arose that it might be the missing young lady in the disguise of an ecclesiastic. The bargello reported to the Vicar-General the failure of his men, as well as the account given by the spy, and the Prelate, sharing the suspicion of the police, sent to his eminence, our master, requesting him to have the person in question, man or woman, turned out of the palace, unless such persons should happen to be known to his excellency, and therefore above suspicion. Cardinal Acquaviva was made acquainted with these circumstances at nine this morning through the auditor you met in my room, and he promised to have the person sent away unless she belonged to his household.

"According to his promise, the cardinal ordered the palace to be searched, but, in less than a quarter of an hour, the major-domo received orders to stop, and the only reason for these new instructions must be this:

"I am told by the major-domo that at nine o'clock exactly a very handsome, young abbe, whom he immediately judged to be a girl in disguise, asked him to deliver a note to his eminence, and that the cardinal, after reading it, had desired the said abbe be brought to his apartment, which he has not left since. As the order to stop searching the palace was given immediately after the introduction of the abbe to the cardinal, it is easy enough to suppose that this ecclesiastic is no other than the young girl missed by the police, who took refuge in the palace in which she must have passed the whole night."

"I suppose," said I, "that his eminence will give her up to-day, if not to the bargello, at least to the Vicar-General."

"No, not even to the Pope himself," answered Gama. "You have not yet a right idea of the protection of our cardinal, and that protection is evidently granted to her, since the young person is not only in the palace of his eminence, but also in his own apartment and under his own guardianship."

The whole affair being in itself very interesting, my attention could not appear extraordinary to Gama, however suspicious he might be naturally, and I was certain that he would not have told me anything if he had guessed the share I had taken in the adventure, and the interest I must have felt in it.

The next day, Gama came to my room with a radiant countenance, and informed me that the Cardinal-Vicar was aware of the ravisher being my friend, and supposed that I was likewise the friend of the girl, as she was the daughter of my French teacher. "Everybody," he added, "is satisfied that you knew the whole affair, and it is natural to suspect that the poor girl spent the night in your room. I admire your prudent reserve during our conversation of yesterday. You kept so well on your guard that I would have sworn you knew nothing whatever of the affair."

"And it is the truth," I answered, very seriously; "I have only learned all the circumstances from you this moment. I know the girl, but I have not seen her for six weeks, since I gave up my French lessons; I am much better acquainted with the young man, but he never confided his project to me. However, people may believe whatever they please. You say that it is natural for the girl to have passed the night in my room, but you will not mind my laughing in the face of those who accept their own suppositions as realities."

"That, my dear friend," said the abbe, "is one of the vices of the Romans; happy those who can afford to laugh at it; but this slander may do you harm, even in the mind of our cardinal."

As there was no performance at the Opera that night, I went to the cardinal's reception; I found no difference towards me either in the cardinal's manners, or in those of any other person, and the marchioness was even more gracious than usual.

After dinner, on the following day, Gama informed me that the cardinal had sent the young girl to a convent in which she would be well treated at his eminence's expense, and that he was certain that she would leave it only to become the wife of the young doctor.

"I should be very happy if it should turn out so," I replied; "for they are both most estimable people."

Two days afterwards, I called upon Father Georgi, and he told me, with an air of sorrow, that the great news of the day in Rome was the failure of the attempt to carry off Dalacqua's daughter, and that all the honour of the intrigue was given to me, which displeased him much. I told him what I had already told Gama, and he appeared to believe me, but he added that in Rome people did not want to know things as they truly were, but only as they wished them to be.

"It is known, that you have been in the habit of going every morning to Dalacqua's house; it is known that the young man often called on you; that is quite enough. People do not care, to know the circumstances which might counteract the slander, but only those, likely to give it new force for slander is vastly relished in the Holy City. Your innocence will not prevent the whole adventure being booked to your account, if, in forty years time you were proposed as pope in the conclave."

During the following days the fatal adventure began to cause me more annoyance than I could express, for everyone mentioned it to me, and I could see clearly that people pretended to believe what I said only because they did not dare to do otherwise. The marchioness told me jeeringly that the Signora Dalacqua had contracted peculiar obligations towards me, but my sorrow was very great when, during the last days of the carnival, I remarked that Cardinal Acquaviva's manner had become constrained, although I was the only person who observed the change.

The noise made by the affair was, however, beginning to subside, when, in the first days of Lent, the cardinal desired me to come to his private room, and spoke as follows:

"The affair of the girl Dalacqua is now over; it is no longer spoken of, but the verdict of the public is that you and I have profited by the clumsiness of the young man who intended to carry her off. In reality I care little for such a verdict, for, under similar circumstances, I should always act in a similar manner, and I do not wish to know that which no one can compel you to confess, and which, as a man of honour, you must not admit. If you had no previous knowledge of the intrigue, and had actually turned the girl out of your room (supposing she did come to you), you would have been guilty of a wrong and cowardly action, because you would have sealed her misery for the remainder of her days, and it would not have caused you to escape the suspicion of being an accomplice, while at the same time it would have attached to you the odium of dastardly treachery. Notwithstanding all I have just said, you can easily imagine that, in spite of my utter contempt for all gossiping fools, I cannot openly defy them. I therefore feel myself compelled to ask you not only to quit my service, but even to leave Rome. I undertake to supply you with an honourable pretext for your departure, so as to insure you the continuation of the respect which you may have secured through the marks of esteem I have bestowed upon you. I promise you to whisper in the ear of any person you may choose, and even to inform everybody, that you are going on an important mission which I have entrusted to you. You have only to name the country where you want to go; I have friends everywhere, and can recommend you to such purpose that you will be sure to find employment. My letters of recommendation will be in my own handwriting, and nobody need know where you are going. Meet me to-morrow at the Villa Negroni, and let me know where my letters are to be addressed. You must be ready to start within a week. Believe me, I am sorry to lose you; but the sacrifice is forced upon me by the most absurd prejudice. Go now, and do not let me witness your grief."

He spoke the last words because he saw my eyes filling with tears, and he did not give me time to answer. Before leaving his room, I had the strength of mind to compose myself, and I put on such an air of cheerfulness that the Abbe Gama, who took me to his room to drink some coffee, complimented me upon my happy looks.

"I am sure," he said, "that they are caused by the conversation you have had with his eminence."

"You are right; but you do not know the sorrow at my heart which I try not to shew outwardly."

"What sorrow?"

"I am afraid of failing in a difficult mission which the cardinal has entrusted me with this morning. I am compelled to conceal how little confidence I feel in myself in order not to lessen the good opinion his eminence is pleased to entertain of me."

"If my advice can be of any service to you, pray dispose of me; but you are quite right to chew yourself calm and cheerful. Is it any business to transact in Rome?"

"No; it is a journey I shall have to undertake in a week or ten days."

"Which way?"

"Towards the west."

"Oh! I am not curious to know."

I went out alone and took a walk in the Villa Borghese, where I spent two hours wrapped in dark despair. I liked Rome, I was on the high road to fortune, and suddenly I found myself in the abyss, without knowing where to go, and with all my hopes scattered to the winds. I examined my conduct, I judged myself severely, I could not find myself guilty of any crime save of too much kindness, but I perceived how right the good Father Georgi had been. My duty was not only to take no part in the intrigue of the two love, but also to change my French teacher the moment I beard of it; but this was like calling in a doctor after death has struck the patient. Besides, young as I was, having no experience yet of misfortune, and still less of the wickedness of society, it was very difficult for me to have that prudence which a man gains only by long intercourse with the world.

"Where shall I go?" This was the question which seemed to me impossible of solution. I thought of it all through the night, and through the morning, but I thought in vain; after Rome, I was indifferent where I went to!

In the evening, not caring for any supper, I had gone to my room; the Abbe Gama came to me with a request from the cardinal not to accept any invitation to dinner for the next day, as he wanted to speak to me.

I therefore waited upon his eminence the next day at the Villa Negroni; he was walking with his secretary, whom he dismissed the moment he saw me. As soon as we were alone, I gave him all the particulars of the intrigue of the two lovers, and I expressed in the most vivid manner the sorrow I felt at leaving his service.

"I have no hope of success," I added, "for I am certain that Fortune will smile upon me only as long as I am near your eminence."

For nearly an hour I told him all the grief with which my heart was bursting, weeping bitterly; yet I could not move him from his decision. Kindly, but firmly he pressed me to tell him to what part of Europe I wanted to go, and despair as much as vexation made me name Constantinople.

"Constantinople!" he exclaimed, moving back a step or two.

"Yes, monsignor, Constantinople," I repeated, wiping away my tears.

The prelate, a man of great wit, but a Spaniard to the very back-bone, after remaining silent a few minutes, said, with a smile,

"I am glad you have not chosen Ispahan, as I should have felt rather embarrassed. When do you wish to go?"

"This day week, as your eminence has ordered me."

"Do you intend to sail from Naples or from Venice?"

"From Venice."

"I will give you such a passport as will be needed, for you will find two armies in winter-quarters in the Romagna. It strikes me that you may tell everybody that I sent you to Constantinople, for nobody will believe you."

This diplomatic suggestion nearly made me smile. The cardinal told me that I should dine with him, and he left me to join his secretary.

When I returned to the palace, thinking of the choice I had made, I said to myself, "Either I am mad, or I am obeying the impulse of a mysterious genius which sends me to Constantinople to work out my fate." I was only astonished that the cardinal had so readily accepted my choice. "Without any doubt," I thought, "he did not wish me to believe that he had boasted of more than he could achieve, in telling me that he had friends everywhere. But to whom can he recommend me in Constantinople? I have not the slightest idea, but to Constantinople I must go."

I dined alone with his eminence; he made a great show of peculiar kindness and I of great satisfaction, for my self-pride, stronger even than my sorrow, forbade me to let anyone guess that I was in disgrace.

My deepest grief was, however, to leave the marchioness, with whom I was in love, and from whom I had not obtained any important favour.

Two days afterwards, the cardinal gave me a passport for Venice, and a sealed letter addressed to Osman Bonneval, Pacha of Caramania, in Constantinople. There was no need of my saying anything to anyone, but, as the cardinal had not forbidden me to do it, I shewed the address on the letter to all my acquaintances.

The Chevalier de Lezze, the Venetian Ambassador, gave me a letter for a wealthy Turk, a very worthy man who had been his friend; Don Gaspar and Father Georgi asked me to write to them, but the Abbe Gams, laughed, and said he was quite sure I was not going to Constantinople.

I went to take my farewell of Donna Cecilia, who had just received a letter from Lucrezia, imparting the news that she would soon be a mother. I also called upon Angelique and Don Francisco, who had lately been married and had not invited me to the wedding.

When I called to take Cardinal Acquaviva's final instructions he gave me a purse containing one hundred ounces, worth seven hundred sequins. I had three hundred more, so that my fortune amounted to one thousand sequins; I kept two hundred, and for the rest I took a letter of exchange upon a Ragusan who was established in Ancona. I left Rome in the coach with a lady going to Our Lady of Loretto, to fulfil a vow made during a severe illness of her daughter, who accompanied her. The young lady was ugly; my journey was a rather tedious one.

IV

MY SHORT BUT RATHER TOO GAY VISIT TO ANCONA—CECILIA,
MARINA, BELLINO—THE GREEK SLAVE OF THE
LAZZARETTO—BELLINO DISCOVERS HIMSELF

I arrived in Ancona on the 25th of February, 1744, and put up at the best inn. Pleased with my room, I told mine host to prepare for me a good meat dinner; but he answered that during Lent all good Catholics eat nothing but fish.

"The Holy Father has granted me permission to eat meat."

"Let me see your permission."

"He gave it to me by word of mouth."

"Reverend sir, I am not obliged to believe you."

"You are a fool."

"I am master in my own house, and I beg you will go to some other inn."

Such an answer, coupled to a most unexpected notice to quit, threw me into a violent passion. I was swearing, raving, screaming, when suddenly a grave-looking individual made his appearance in my room, and said to me:

"Sir, you are wrong in calling for meat, when in Ancona fish is much better; you are wrong in expecting the landlord to believe you on your bare word; and if you have obtained the permission from the Pope, you have been wrong in soliciting it at your age; you have been wrong in not asking for such permission in writing; you are wrong in calling the host a fool, because it is a compliment that no man is likely to accept in his own house; and, finally, you are wrong in making such an uproar."

Far from increasing my bad temper, this individual, who had entered my room only to treat me to a sermon, made me laugh.

"I willingly plead guilty, sir," I answered, "to all the counts which you allege against me; but it is raining, it is getting late, I am tired and hungry, and therefore you will easily understand that I do not feel disposed to change my quarters. Will you give me some supper, as the landlord refuses to do so?"

"No," he replied, with great composure, "because I am a good Catholic and fast. But I will undertake to make it all right for you with the landlord, who will give you a good supper."

Thereupon he went downstairs, and I, comparing my hastiness to his calm, acknowledged the man worthy of teaching me some lessons. He soon came up again, informed me that peace was signed, and that I would be served immediately.

"Will you not take supper with me?"

"No, but I will keep you company."

I accepted his offer, and to learn who he was, I told him my name, giving myself the title of secretary to Cardinal Acquaviva.

"My name is Sancio Pico," he said; "I am a Castilian, and the 'proveditore' of the army of H. C. M., which is commanded by Count de Gages under the orders of the generalissimo, the Duke of Modem."

My excellent appetite astonished him, and he enquired whether I had dined. "No," said I; and I saw his countenance assume an air of satisfaction.

"Are you not afraid such a supper will hurt you?" he said.

"On the contrary, I hope it will do me a great deal of good."

"Then you have deceived the Pope?"

"No, for I did not tell him that I had no appetite, but only that I liked meat better than fish."

"If you feel disposed to hear some good music," he said a moment after, "follow me to the next room; the prima donna of Ancona lives there."

The words prima donna interested me at once, and I followed him. I saw, sitting before a table, a woman already somewhat advanced in age, with two young girls and two boys, but I looked in vain for the actress, whom Don Sancio Pico at last presented to me in the shape of one of the two boys, who was remarkably handsome and might have been seventeen. I thought he was a 'castrato' who, as is the custom in Rome, performed all the parts of a prima donna. The mother presented to, me her other son, likewise very good-looking, but more manly than the 'castrato', although younger. His name was Petronio, and, keeping up the transformations of the family, he was the first female dancer at the opera. The eldest girl, who was also introduced to me, was named Cecilia, and studied music; she was twelve years old; the youngest, called Marina, was only eleven, and like her brother Petronio was consecrated to the worship of Terpsichore. Both the girls were very pretty.

The family came from Bologna and lived upon the talent of its members; cheerfulness and amiability replaced wealth with them. Bellino, such was the name of the castrato, yielding to the entreaties of

Don Sancio, rose from the table, went to the harpiscord, and sang with the voice of an angel and with delightful grace. The Castilian listened with his eyes closed in an ecstasy of enjoyment, but I, far from closing my eyes, gazed into Bellino's, which seemed to dart amorous lightnings upon me. I could discover in him some of the features of Lucrezia and the graceful manner of the marchioness, and everything betrayed a beautiful woman, for his dress concealed but imperfectly the most splendid bosom. The consequence was that, in spite of his having been introduced as a man, I fancied that the so-called Bellino was a disguised beauty, and, my imagination taking at once the highest flight, I became thoroughly enamoured.

We spent two very pleasant hours, and I returned to my room accompanied by the Castilian. "I intend to leave very early to-morrow morning," he said, "for Sinigaglia, with the Abbe Vilmarcati, but I expect to return for supper the day after to-morrow." I wished him a happy journey, saying that we would most 'likely meet on the road, as I should probably leave Ancona myself on the same day, after paying a visit to my banker.

I went to bed thinking of Bellino and of the impression he had made upon me; I was sorry to go away without having proved to him that I was not the dupe of his disguise. Accordingly, I was well pleased to see him enter my room in the morning as soon as I had opened my door. He came to offer me the services of his young brother Petronio during my stay in Ancona, instead of my engaging a valet de place. I willingly agreed to the proposal, and sent Petronio to get coffee for all the family.

I asked Bellino to sit on my bed with the intention of making love to him, and of treating him like a girl, but the two young sisters ran into my room and disturbed my plans. Yet the trio formed before me a very pleasing sight; they represented natural beauty and artless cheerfulness of three different kinds; unobtrusive familiarity, theatrical wit, pleasing playfulness, and pretty Bolognese manners which I witnessed for the first time; all this would have sufficed to cheer me if I had been downcast. Cecilia and Marina were two sweet rosebuds, which, to bloom in all their beauty, required only the inspiration of love, and they would certainly have had the preference over Bellino if I had seen in him only the miserable outcast of mankind, or rather the pitiful victim of sacerdotal cruelty, for, in spite of their youth, the two amiable girls offered on their dawning bosom the precious image of womanhood.

Petronio came with the coffee which he poured out, and I sent some to the mother, who never left her room. Petronio was a true male harlot by taste and by profession. The species is not scare in Italy, where the offence is not regarded with the wild and ferocious intolerance of England and Spain. I had given him one sequin to pay for the coffee, and told him to keep the change, and, to chew me his gratitude, he gave me a voluptuous kiss with half-open lips, supposing in me a taste which I was very far from entertaining. I disabused him, but he did not seem the least ashamed. I told him to order dinner for six persons, but he remarked that he would order it only for four, as he had to keep his dear mother company; she always took her dinner in bed. Everyone to his taste, I thought, and I let him do as he pleased.

Two minutes after he had gone, the landlord came to my room and said, "Reverend sir, the persons you have invited here have each the appetite of two men at least; I give you notice of it, because I must charge accordingly." "All right," I replied, "but let us have a good dinner."

When I was dressed, I thought I ought to pay my compliments to the compliant mother. I went to her room, and congratulated her upon her children. She thanked me for the present I had given to Petronio, and began to make me the confidant of her distress. "The manager of the theatre," she said, "is a miser who has given us only fifty Roman crowns for the whole carnival. We have spent them for our living, and, to return to Bologna, we shall have to walk and beg our way." Her confidence moved my pity, so I took a gold quadruple from my purse and offered it to her; she wept for joy and gratitude.

"I promise you another gold quadruple, madam," I said, "if you will confide in me entirely. Confess that Bellino is a pretty woman in disguise."

"I can assure you it is not so, although he has the appearance of a woman."

"Not only the appearance, madam, but the tone, the manners; I am a good judge."

"Nevertheless, he is a boy, for he has had to be examined before he could sing on the stage here."

"And who examined him?"

"My lord bishop's chaplain."

"A chaplain?"

"Yes, and you may satisfy yourself by enquiring from him."

"The only way to clear my doubts would be to examine him myself."

"You may, if he has no objection, but truly I cannot interfere, as I do not know what your intentions are."

"They are quite natural."

I returned to my room and sent Petronio for a bottle of Cyprus wine. He brought the wine and seven sequins, the change for the doubloon I had given him. I divided them between Bellino, Cecilia and Marina, and begged the two young girls to leave me alone with their brother.

"Bellino, I am certain that your natural conformation is different from mine; my dear, you are a girl."

"I am a man, but a castrato; I have been examined."

"Allow me to examine you likewise, and I will give you a doubloon."

"I cannot, for it is evident that you love me, and such love is condemned by religion."

"You did not raise these objections with the bishop's chaplain."

"He was an elderly priest, and besides, he only just glanced at me."

"I will know the truth," said I, extending my hand boldly.

But he repulsed me and rose from his chair. His obstinacy vexed me, for I had already spent fifteen or sixteen sequins to satisfy my curiosity.

I began my dinner with a very bad humour, but the excellent appetite of my pretty guests brought me round, and I soon thought that, after all, cheerfulness was better than sulking, and I resolved to make up for my disappointment with the two charming sisters, who seemed well disposed to enjoy a frolic.

I began by distributing a few innocent kisses right and left, as I sat between them near a good fire, eating chestnuts which we wetted with Cyprus wine. But very soon my greedy hands touched every part which my lips could not kiss, and Cecilia, as well as Marina, delighted in the game. Seeing that Bellino was smiling, I kissed him likewise, and his half-open ruffle attracting my hand, I ventured and went in without resistance. The chisel of Praxiteles had never carved a finer bosom!

"Oh! this is enough," I exclaimed; "I can no longer doubt that you are a beautifully-formed woman!"

"It is," he replied, "the defect of all castrati."

"No, it is the perfection of all handsome women. Bellino, believe me, I am enough of a good judge to distinguish between the deformed breast of a castrato, and that of a beautiful woman; and your alabaster bosom belongs to a young beauty of seventeen summers."

Who does not know that love, inflamed by all that can excite it, never stops in young people until it is satisfied, and that one favour granted kindles the wish for a greater one? I had begun well, I tried to go further and to smother with burning kisses that which my hand was pressing so ardently, but the false Bellino, as if he had only just been aware of the illicit pleasure I was enjoying, rose and ran away. Anger increased in me the ardour of love, and feeling the necessity of calming myself either by satisfying my ardent desires or by evaporating them, I begged Cecilia, Bellino's pupil, to sing a few Neapolitan airs.

I then went out to call upon the banker, from whom I took a letter of exchange at sight upon Bologna, for the amount I had to receive from him, and on my return, after a light supper with the two young sisters, I prepared to go to bed, having previously instructed Petronio to order a carriage for the morning.

I was just locking my door when Cecilia, half undressed, came in to say that Bellino begged me to take him to Rimini, where he was engaged to sing in an opera to be performed after Easter.

"Go and tell him, my dear little seraph, that I am ready to do what he wishes, if he will only grant me in your presence what I desire; I want to know for a certainty whether he is a man or a woman."

She left me and returned soon, saying that Bellino had gone to bed, but that if I would postpone my departure for one day only he promised to satisfy me on the morrow.

"Tell me the truth, Cecilia, and I will give you six sequins."

"I cannot earn them, for I have never seen him naked, and I cannot swear to his being a girl. But he must be a man, otherwise he would not have been allowed to perform here."

"Well, I will remain until the day after to-morrow, provided you keep me company tonight."

"Do you love me very much?"

"Very much indeed, if you shew yourself very kind."

"I will be very kind, for I love you dearly likewise. I will go and tell my mother."

"Of course you have a lover?"

"I never had one."

She left my room, and in a short time came back full of joy, saying that her mother believed me an honest man; she of course meant a generous one. Cecilia locked the door, and throwing herself in my arms covered me with kisses. She was pretty, charming, but I was not in love with her, and I was not able to say to her as to Lucrezia: "You have made me so happy!" But she said it herself, and I did not feel much flattered, although I pretended to believe her. When I woke up in the morning I gave her a tender salutation, and presenting her with three doubloons, which must have particularly delighted the mother, I sent her away without losing my time in promising everlasting constancy—a promise as absurd as it is trifling, and which the most virtuous man ought never to make even to the most beautiful of women.

After breakfast I sent for mine host and ordered an excellent supper for five persons, feeling certain that Don Sancio, whom I expected in the evening, would not refuse to honour me by accepting my invitation, and with that idea I made up my mind to go without my dinner. The Bolognese family did not require to imitate my diet to insure a good appetite for the evening.

I then summoned Bellino to my room, and claimed the performance of his promise but he laughed, remarked that the day was not passed yet, and said that he was certain of traveling with me.

"I fairly warn you that you cannot accompany me unless I am fully satisfied."

"Well, I will satisfy you."

"Shall we go and take a walk together?"

"Willingly; I will dress myself."

While I was waiting for him, Marina came in with a dejected countenance, enquiring how she had deserved my contempt.

"Cecilia has passed the night with you, Bellino will go with you to-morrow, I am the most unfortunate of us all."

"Do you want money?"

"No, for I love you."

"But, Marinetta, you are too young."

"I am much stronger than my sister."

"Perhaps you have a lover."

"Oh! no."

"Very well, we can try this evening."

"Good! Then I will tell mother to prepare clean sheets for to-morrow morning; otherwise everybody here would know that I slept with you."

I could not help admiring the fruits of a theatrical education, and was much amused.

Bellino came back, we went out together, and we took our walk towards the harbour. There were several vessels at anchor, and amongst them a Venetian ship and a Turkish tartan. We went on board the first which we visited with interest, but not seeing anyone of my acquaintance, we rowed towards the Turkish tartan, where the most romantic surprise awaited me. The first person I met on board was the beautiful Greek woman I had left in Ancona, seven months before, when I went away from the lazzaretto. She was seated near the old captain, of whom I enquired, without appearing to notice his handsome slave, whether he had any fine goods to sell. He took us to his cabin, but as I cast a glance towards the charming Greek, she expressed by her looks all her delight at such an unexpected meeting.

I pretended not to be pleased with the goods shewn by the Turk, and under the impulse of inspiration I told him that I would willingly buy something pretty which would take the fancy of his better-half. He smiled, and the Greek slave-having whispered a few words to him, he left the cabin. The moment he was out of sight, this new Aspasia threw herself in my arms, saying, "Now is your time!" I would not be found wanting in courage, and taking the most convenient position in such a place, I did to her in one instant that which her old master had not done in five years. I had not yet reached the goal of my wishes, when the unfortunate girl, hearing her master, tore herself from my arms with a deep sigh, and placing herself cunningly in front of me, gave me time to repair the disorder of my dress, which might have cost me my life, or at least all I possessed to compromise the affair. In that curious situation, I was highly amused at the surprise of Bellino, who stood there trembling like an aspen leaf.

The trifles chosen by the handsome slave cost me only thirty sequins. 'Spolaitis', she said to me in her own language, and the Turk telling her that she ought to kiss me, she covered her face with her hands, and ran away. I left the ship more sad than pleased, for I regretted that, in spite of her courage, she should have enjoyed only an incomplete pleasure. As soon as we were in our row boat, Bellino, who had recovered from his fright, told me that I had just made him acquainted with a phenomenon, the reality of which he could not admit, and which gave him a very strange idea of my nature; that, as far as the Greek girl was concerned, he could not make her out, unless I should assure him that every woman in her country was like her. "How unhappy they must be!" he added.

"Do you think," I asked, "that coquettes are happier?"

"No, but I think that when a woman yields to love, she should not be conquered before she has fought with her own desires; she should not give way to the first impulse of a lustful desire and abandon herself to the first man who takes her fancy, like an animal—the slave of sense. You must confess that the Greek woman has given you an evident proof that you had taken her fancy, but that she has at the same time given you a proof not less certain of her beastly lust, and of an effrontery which exposed her to the shame of being repulsed, for she could not possibly know whether you would feel as well disposed for her as she felt for you. She is very handsome, and it all turned out well, but the adventure has thrown me into a whirlpool of agitation which I cannot yet control."

I might easily have put a stop to Bellino's perplexity, and rectified the mistake he was labouring under; but such a confession would not have ministered to my self-love, and I held my peace, for, if Bellino happened to be a girl, as I suspected, I wanted her to be convinced that I attached, after all, but very little importance to the great affair, and that it was not worth while employing cunning expedients to obtain it.

We returned to the inn, and, towards evening, hearing Don Sancio's travelling carriage roll into the yard, I hastened to meet him, and told him that I hoped he would excuse me if I had felt certain that he would not refuse me the honour of his company to supper with Bellino. He thanked me politely for the pleasure I was so delicately offering him, and accepted my invitation.

The most exquisite dishes, the most delicious wines of Spain, and, more than everything else, the cheerfulness and the charming voices of Bellino and of Cecilia, gave the Castilian five delightful hours. He left me at midnight, saying that he could not declare himself thoroughly pleased unless I promised to sup with him the next evening with the same guests. It would compel me to postpone my departure for another day, but I accepted.

As soon as Don Sancio had gone, I called upon Bellino to fulfil his promise, but he answered that Marinetta was waiting for me, and that, as I was not going away the next day, he would find an opportunity of satisfying my doubts; and wishing me a good night, he left the room.

Marinetta, as cheerful as a lark, ran to lock the door and came back to me, her eyes beaming with ardour. She was more formed than Cecilia, although one year younger, and seemed anxious to convince me of her superiority, but, thinking that the fatigue of the preceding night might have exhausted my strength, she unfolded all the amorous ideas of her mind, explained at length all she knew of the great mystery she was going to enact with me, and of all the contrivances she had had recourse to in order to acquire her imperfect knowledge, the whole interlarded with the foolish talk natural to her age. I made out that she was afraid of my not finding her a maiden, and of my reproaching her about it. Her anxiety pleased me, and I gave her a new confidence by telling her that nature had refused to many young girls what is called maidenhood, and that only a fool could be angry with a girl for such a reason.

My science gave her courage and confidence, and I was compelled to acknowledge that she was very superior to her sister.

"I am delighted you find me so," she said; "we must not sleep at all throughout the night."

"Sleep, my darling, will prove our friend, and our strength renewed by repose will reward you in the morning for what you may suppose lost time."

And truly, after a quiet sleep, the morning was for her a succession of fresh triumphs, and I crowned her happiness by sending her away with three doubloons, which she took to her mother, and which gave the good woman an insatiable desire to contract new obligations towards Providence.

I went out to get some money from the banker, as I did not know what might happen during my journey. I had enjoyed myself, but I had spent too much: yet there was Bellino who, if a girl, was not to find me less generous than I had been with the two young sisters. It was to be decided during the day, and I fancied that I was sure of the result.

There are some persons who pretend that life is only a succession of misfortunes, which is as much as to say that life itself is a misfortune; but if life is a misfortune, death must be exactly the reverse and therefore death must be happiness, since death is the very reverse of life. That deduction may appear too finely drawn. But those who say that life is a succession of misfortunes are certainly either ill or poor; for, if they enjoyed good health, if they had cheerfulness in their heart and money in their purse, if they had for their enjoyment a Cecilia, a Marinetta, and even a more lovely beauty in perspective, they would soon entertain a very different opinion of life! I hold them to be a race of pessimists, recruited amongst beggarly philosophers and knavish, atrabilious theologians. If pleasure does exist, and if life is necessary to enjoy pleasure, then life is happiness. There are misfortunes, as I know by experience; but the very existence of such misfortunes proves that the sum-total of happiness is greater. Because a few thorns are to be found in a basket full of roses, is the existence of those beautiful flowers to be denied? No; it is a slander to deny that life is happiness. When I am in a dark room, it pleases me greatly to see through a window an immense horizon before me.

As supper-time was drawing near, I went to Don Sancio, whom I found in magnificently-furnished apartments. The table was loaded with silver plate, and his servants were in livery. He was alone, but all his guests arrived soon after me—Cecilia, Marina, and Bellino, who, either by caprice or from taste, was dressed as a woman. The two young sisters, prettily arranged, looked charming, but Bellino, in his female costume, so completely threw them into the shade, that my last doubt vanished.

"Are you satisfied," I said to Don Sancio, "that Bellino is a woman?"

"Woman or man, what do I care! I think he is a very pretty 'castrato', and 'I have seen many as good-looking as he is."

"But are you sure he is a 'castrato'?"

"'Valgame Dios'!" answered the grave Castilian, "I have not the slightest wish to ascertain the truth."

Oh, how widely different our thoughts were! I admired in him the wisdom of which I was so much in need, and did not venture upon any more indiscreet questions. During the supper, however, my greedy eyes could not leave that charming being; my vicious nature caused me to feel intense voluptuousness in believing him to be of that sex to which I wanted him to belong.

Don Sancio's supper was excellent, and, as a matter of course, superior to mine; otherwise the pride of the Castilian would have felt humbled. As a general rule, men are not satisfied with what is good; they want the best, or, to speak more to the point, the most. He gave us white truffles, several sorts of shell-fish, the best fish of the Adriatic, dry champagne, peralta, sherry and pedroximenes wines.

After that supper worthy of Lucullus, Bellino sang with a voice of such beauty that it deprived us of the small amount of reason left in us by the excellent wine. His movements, the expression of his looks, his gait, his walk, his countenance, his voice, and, above all, my own instinct, which told me that I could not possibly feel for a castrato what I felt for Bellino, confirmed me in my hopes; yet it was necessary that my eyes should ascertain the truth.

After many compliments and a thousand thanks, we took leave of the grand Spaniard, and went to my room, where the mystery was at last to be unravelled. I called upon Bellino to keep his word, or I threatened to leave him alone the next morning at day-break.

I took him by the hand, and we seated ourselves near the fire. I dismissed Cecilia and Marina, and I said to him,

"Bellino, everything must have an end; you have promised: it will soon be over. If you are what you represent yourself to be, I will let you go back to your own room; if you are what I believe you to be, and if you consent to remain with me to-night, I will give you one hundred sequins, and we will start together tomorrow morning."

"You must go alone, and forgive me if I cannot fulfil my promise. I am what I told you, and I can neither reconcile myself to the idea of exposing my shame before you, nor lay myself open to the terrible consequences that might follow the solution of your doubts."

"There can be no consequences, since there will be an end to it at the moment I have assured myself that you are unfortunate enough to be what you say, and without ever mentioning the circumstances again, I promise to take you with me to-morrow and to leave you at Rimini."

"No, my mind is made up; I cannot satisfy your curiosity."

Driven to madness by his words, I was very near using violence, but subduing my angry feelings, I endeavored to succeed by gentle means and by going straight to the spot where the mystery could be solved. I was very near it, when his hand opposed a very strong resistance. I repeated my efforts, but Bellino, rising suddenly, repulsed me, and I found myself undone. After a few moments of calm, thinking I should take him by surprise, I extended my hand, but I drew back terrified, for I fancied that I had recognized in him a man, and a degraded man, contemptible less on account of his degradation than for the want of feeling I thought I could read on his countenance. Disgusted, confused, and almost blushing for myself, I sent him away.

His sisters came to my room, but I dismissed them, sending word to their brother that he might go with me, without any fear of further indiscretion on my part. Yet, in spite of the conviction I thought I had acquired, Bellino, even such as I believe him to be, filled my thoughts; I could not make it out.

Early the next morning I left Ancona with him, distracted by the tears of the two charming sisters and loaded with the blessings of the mother who, with beads in hand, mumbled her 'paternoster', and repeated her constant theme: 'Dio provedera'.

The trust placed in Providence by most of those persons who earn their living by some profession forbidden by religion is neither absurd, nor false, nor deceitful; it is real and even godly, for it flows from an excellent source. Whatever may be the ways of Providence, human beings must always acknowledge it in its action, and those who call upon Providence independently of all external consideration must, at the bottom, be worthy, although guilty of transgressing its laws.

> 'Pulchra Laverna,
> Da mihi fallere; da justo sanctoque videri;
> Noctem peccati, et fraudibus objice nubem.'

Such was the way in which, in the days of Horace, robbers addressed their goddess, and I recollect a Jesuit who told me once that Horace would not have known his own language, if he had said justo sanctoque: but there were ignorant men even amongst the Jesuits, and robbers most likely have but little respect for the rules of grammar.

The next morning I started with Bellino, who, believing me to be undeceived, could suppose that I would not shew any more curiosity about him, but we had not been a quarter of an hour together when he found out his mistake, for I could not let my looks fall upon his splendid eyes without feeling in me a fire which the sight of a man could not have ignited. I told him that all his features were those of a woman, and that I wanted the testimony of my eyes before I could feel perfectly satisfied, because the protuberance I had felt in a certain place might be only a freak of nature. "Should it be the case," I added, "I should have no difficulty in passing over a deformity which, in reality, is only laughable. Bellino, the impression you produce upon me, this sort of magnetism, your bosom worthy of Venus herself, which you have once abandoned to my eager hand, the sound of your voice, every movement of yours, assure me that you do not belong to my sex. Let me see for myself, and, if my conjectures are right, depend upon my faithful love; if, on the contrary, I find that I have been mistaken, you can rely upon my friendship. If you refuse me, I shall be compelled to believe that you are cruelly enjoying my misery, and that you have learned in the most accursed school that the best way of preventing a young man from curing himself of an amorous passion is to excite it constantly; but you must agree with me that, to put such tyranny in practice, it is necessary to hate the person it is practised upon, and, if that be so, I ought to call upon my reason to give me the strength necessary to hate you likewise."

I went on speaking for a long time; Bellino did not answer, but he seemed deeply moved. At last I told him that, in the fearful state to which I was reduced by his resistance, I should be compelled to treat him without any regard for his feelings, and find out the truth by force. He answered with much warmth and dignity: "Recollect that you are not my master, that I am in your hands, because I had faith in your promise, and that, if you use violence, you will be guilty of murder. Order the postillion to stop, I will get out of the carriage, and you may rely upon my not complaining of your treatment."

Those few words were followed by a torrent of tears, a sight which I never could resist. I felt myself moved in the inmost recesses of my soul, and I almost thought that I had been wrong. I say almost, because, had I been convinced of it, I would have thrown myself at his feet entreating pardon; but, not feeling myself competent to stand in judgment in my own cause, I satisfied myself by remaining dull and silent, and I never uttered one word until we were only half a mile from Sinigaglia, where I intended to take supper and to remain for the night. Having fought long enough with my own feelings, I said to him;

"We might have spent a little time in Rimini like good friends, if you had felt any friendship for me, for, with a little kind compliance, you could have easily cured me of my passion."

"It would not cure you," answered Bellino, courageously, but with a sweetness of tone which surprised me; "no, you would not be cured, whether you found me to be man or woman, for you are in love with me independently of my sex, and the certainty you would acquire would make you furious. In such a state, should you find me inexorable, you would very likely give way to excesses which would afterwards cause you deep sorrow."

"You expect to make me admit that you are right, but you are completely mistaken, for I feel that I should remain perfectly calm, and that by complying with my wishes you would gain my friendship."

"I tell you again that you would become furious."

"Bellino, that which has made me furious is the sight of your charms, either too real or too completely deceiving, the power of which you cannot affect to ignore. You have not been afraid to ignite my amorous fury, how can you expect me to believe you now, when you pretend to fear it, and when I am only asking you to let me touch a thing, which, if it be as you say, will only disgust me?"

"Ah! disgust you; I am quite certain of the contrary. Listen to me. Were I a girl, I feel I could not resist loving you, but, being a man, it is my duty not to grant what you desire, for your passion, now very natural, would then become monstrous. Your ardent nature would be stronger than your reason, and your reason itself would easily come to the assistance of your senses and of your nature. That violent clearing-up of the mystery, were you to obtain it, would leave you deprived of all control over yourself. Disappointed in not finding what you had expected, you would satisfy your passion upon that which you would find, and the result would, of course, be an abomination. How can you, intelligent as you are, flatter yourself that, finding me to be a man, you could all at once cease to love me? Would the charms which you now see in me cease to exist then? Perhaps their power would, on the contrary, be enhanced, and your passion, becoming brutal, would lead you to take any means your imagination suggested to gratify it. You would persuade yourself that you might change me into a woman, or, what is worse, that you might change yourself into one. Your passion would invent a thousand sophisms to justify your love, decorated with the fine appellation of friendship, and you would not fail to allege hundreds of similarly disgusting cases in order to excuse your conduct. You would certainly never find me compliant; and how am I to know that you would not threaten me with death?"

"Nothing of the sort would happen, Bellino," I answered, rather tired of the length of his argument, "positively nothing, and I am sure you are exaggerating your fears. Yet I am bound to tell you that, even if all you say should happen, it seems to me that to allow what can strictly be considered only as a temporary fit of insanity, would prove a less evil than to render incurable a disease of the mind which reason would soon cut short."

Thus does a poor philosopher reason when he takes it into his head to argue at those periods during which a passion raging in his soul makes all its faculties wander. To reason well, we must be under the sway neither of love nor of anger, for those two passions have one thing in common which is that, in their excess, they lower us to the condition of brutes acting only under the influence of their predominating instinct, and, unfortunately, we are never more disposed to argue than when we feel ourselves under the influence of either of those two powerful human passions.

We arrived at Sinigaglia late at night, and I went to the best inn, and, after choosing a comfortable room, ordered supper. As there was but one bed in the room, I asked Bellino, in as calm a tone as I could assume, whether he would have a fire lighted in another chamber, and my surprise may be imagined when he answered quietly that he had no objection to sleep in the same bed with me. Such an answer, however, unexpected, was necessary to dispel the angry feelings under which I was labouring. I guessed that I was near the denouement of the romance, but I was very far from congratulating myself, for I did not know whether the denouement would prove agreeable or not. I felt, however, a real satisfaction at having conquered, and was sure of my self-control, in case the senses, my natural instinct, led me astray. But if I found myself in the right, I thought I could expect the most precious favours.

We sat down to supper opposite each other, and during the meal, his words, his countenance, the expression of his beautiful eyes, his sweet and voluptuous smile, everything seemed to announce that he had had enough of playing a part which must have proved as painful to him as to me.

A weight was lifted off my mind, and I managed to shorten the supper as much as possible. As soon as we had left the table, my amiable companion called for a night-lamp, undressed himself, and went to bed. I was not long in following him, and the reader will soon know the nature of a denouement so long and so ardently desired; in the mean time I beg to wish him as happy a night as the one which was then awaiting me.

V

Bellino's History—I am Put Under Arrest—I Run Away
Against My Will—My Return to Rimini,
and My Arrival in Bologna

Dear reader, I said enough at the end of the last chapter to make you guess what happened, but no language would be powerful enough to make you realize all the voluptuousness which that charming being had in store for me. She came close to me the moment I was in bed. Without uttering one word our lips met, and I found myself in the ecstasy of enjoyment before I had had time to seek for it. After so complete a victory, what would my eyes and my fingers have gained from investigations which could not give me more certainty than I had already obtained? I could not take my gaze off that beautiful face, which was all aflame with the ardour of love.

After a moment of quiet rapture, a spark lighted up in our veins a fresh conflagration which we drowned in a sea of new delights. Bellino felt bound to make me forget my sufferings, and to reward me by an ardour equal to the fire kindled by her charms.

The happiness I gave her increased mine twofold, for it has always been my weakness to compose the four-fifths of my enjoyment from the sum-total of the happiness which I gave the charming being from whom I derived it. But such a feeling must necessarily cause hatred for old age which can still receive pleasure, but can no longer give enjoyment to another. And youth runs away from old age, because it is its most cruel enemy.

An interval of repose became necessary, in consequence of the activity of our enjoyment. Our senses were not tired out, but they required the rest which renews their sensitiveness and restores the buoyancy necessary to active service.

Bellino was the first to break our silence.

"Dearest," she said, "are you satisfied now? Have you found me truly loving?"

"Truly loving? Ah! traitress that you are! Do you, then, confess that I was not mistaken when I guessed that you were a charming woman? And if you truly loved me, tell me how you could contrive to defer your happiness and mine so long? But is it quite certain that I did not make a mistake?"

GIACOMO CASANOVA

"I am yours all over; see for yourself."

Oh, what delightful survey! what charming beauties! what an ocean of enjoyment! But I could not find any trace of the protuberance which had so much terrified and disgusted me.

"What has become," I said, "of that dreadful monstrosity?"

"Listen to me," she replied, "and I will tell you everything.

"My name is Therese. My father, a poor clerk in the Institute of Bologna, had let an apartment in his house to the celebrated Salimberi, a castrato, and a delightful musician. He was young and handsome, he became attached to me, and I felt flattered by his affection and by the praise he lavished upon me. I was only twelve years of age; he proposed to teach me music, and finding that I had a fine voice, he cultivated it carefully, and in less than a year I could accompany myself on the harpsichord. His reward was that which his love for me induced him to ask, and I granted the reward without feeling any humiliation, for I worshipped him. Of course, men like yourself are much above men of his species, but Salimberi was an exception. His beauty, his manners, his talent, and the rare qualities of his soul, made him superior in my eyes to all the men I had seen until then. He was modest and reserved, rich and generous, and I doubt whether he could have found a woman able to resist him; yet I never heard him boast of having seduced any. The mutilation practised upon his body had made him a monster, but he was an angel by his rare qualities and endowments.

"Salimberi was at that time educating a boy of the same age as myself, who was in Rimini with a music teacher. The father of the boy, who was poor and had a large family, seeing himself near death, had thought of having his unfortunate son maimed so that he should become the support of his brothers with his voice. The name of the boy was Bellino; the good woman whom you have just seen in Ancona was his mother, and everybody believes that she is mine.

"I had belonged to Salimberi for about a year, when he announced to me one day, weeping bitterly, that he was compelled to leave me to go to Rome, but he promised to see me again. The news threw me into despair. He had arranged everything for the continuation of my musical education, but, as he was preparing himself for his departure, my father died very suddenly, after a short illness, and I was left an orphan.

"Salimberi had not courage enough to resist my tears and my entreaties; he made up his mind to take me to Rimini, and to place me in the same house where his young 'protege' was educated. We reached

Rimini, and put up at an inn; after a short rest, Salimberi left me to call upon the teacher of music, and to make all necessary arrangements respecting me with him; but he soon returned, looking sad and unhappy; Bellino had died the day before.

"As he was thinking of the grief which the loss of the young man would cause his mother, he was struck with the idea of bringing me back to Bologna under the name of Bellino, where he could arrange for my board with the mother of the deceased Bellino, who, being very poor, would find it to her advantage to keep the secret. 'I will give her,' he said, 'everything necessary for the completion of your musical education, and in four years, I will take you to Dresden (he was in the service of the Elector of Saxony, King of Poland), not as a girl, but as a castrato. There we will live together without giving anyone cause for scandal, and you will remain with me and minister to my happiness until I die. All we have to do is to represent you as Bellino, and it is very easy, as nobody knows you in Bologna. Bellino's mother will alone know the secret; her other children have seen their brother only when he was very young, and can have no suspicion. But if you love me you must renounce your sex, lose even the remembrance of it, and leave immediately for Bologna, dressed as a boy, and under the name of Bellino. You must be very careful lest anyone should find out that you are a girl; you must sleep alone, dress yourself in private, and when your bosom is formed, as it will be in a year or two, it will only be thought a deformity not uncommon amongst 'castrati'. Besides, before leaving you, I will give you a small instrument, and teach how to fix it in such manner that, if you had at any time to submit to an examination, you would easily be mistaken for a man. If you accept my plan, I feel certain that we can live together in Dresden without losing the good graces of the queen, who is very religious. Tell me, now, whether you will accept my proposal?

"He could not entertain any doubt of my consent, for I adored him. As soon as he had made a boy of me we left Rimini for Bologna, where we arrived late in the evening. A little gold made everything right with Bellino's mother; I gave her the name of mother, and she kissed me, calling me her dear son. Salimberi left us, and returned a short time afterwards with the instrument which would complete my transformation. He taught me, in the presence of my new mother, how to fix it with some tragacanth gum, and I found myself exactly like my friend. I would have laughed at it, had not my heart been deeply grieved at the departure of my beloved Salimberi, for he bade me farewell as soon as the curious operation was completed. People laugh at forebodings; I do not believe in them myself, but the foreboding of evil, which almost broke my heart as he gave me his farewell kiss, did not deceive me. I felt the cold shivering of death run through me; I felt I was looking at him for the last time, and I fainted away. Alas! my fears proved only too prophetic. Salimberi died a year ago in the Tyrol in the prime of life, with the calmness of a true philosopher. His death compelled me to earn my living with the assistance of my musical talent. My mother advised me to continue to give myself out as a castrato, in the hope of being able to take me to Rome. I agreed to do so, for I did not feel sufficient energy to decide upon any other plan. In the meantime she accepted an offer for the Ancona Theatre, and Petronio took the part of first female dancer; in this way we played the comedy of 'The World Turned Upside Down.'

"After Salimberi, you are the only man I have known, and, if you like, you can restore me to my original state, and make me give up the name of Bellino, which I hate since the death of my protector, and which begins to inconvenience me. I have only appeared at two theatres, and each time I have been compelled to submit to the scandalous, degrading examination, because everywhere I am thought to have too much the appearance of a girl, and I am admitted only after the shameful test has brought conviction. Until now, fortunately, I have had to deal only with old priests who, in their good faith, have been satisfied with a very slight examination, and have made a favourable report to the bishop; but I might fall into the hands of some young abbe, and the test would then become a more severe one. Besides, I find myself exposed to the daily persecutions of two sorts of beings: those who, like you, cannot and will not believe me to be a man, and those who, for the satisfaction of their disgusting propensities, are delighted at my being so, or find it advantageous to suppose me so. The last particularly annoy me! Their tastes are so infamous, their habits so low, that I fear I shall murder one of them some day, when I can no longer control the rage in which their obscene language throws me. Out of pity, my beloved angel, be generous; and, if you love me, oh! free me from this state of shame and degradation! Take me with you. I do not ask to become your wife, that would be too much happiness; I will only be your friend, your mistress, as I would have been Salimberi's; my heart is pure and innocent, I feel that I can remain faithful to my lover through my whole life. Do not abandon me. The love I have for you is sincere; my affection for Salimberi was innocent; it was born of my inexperience and of my gratitude, and it is only with you that I have felt myself truly a woman."

Her emotion, an inexpressible charm which seemed to flow from her lips and to enforce conviction, made me shed tears of love and sympathy. I blended my tears with those falling from her beautiful eyes, and deeply moved, I promised not to abandon her and to make her the sharer of my fate. Interested in the history, as singular as extraordinary, that she had just narrated, and having seen nothing in it that did not bear the stamp of truth, I felt really disposed to make her happy but I could not believe that I had inspired her with a very deep passion during my short stay in Ancona, many circumstances of which might, on the contrary, have had an opposite effect upon her heart.

"If you loved me truly," I said, "how could you let me sleep with your sisters, out of spite at your resistance?"

"Alas, dearest! think of our great poverty, and how difficult it was for me to discover myself. I loved you; but was it not natural that I should suppose your inclination for me only a passing caprice? When I saw you go so easily from Cecilia to Marinetta, I thought that you would treat me in the same manner as soon as your desires were satisfied, I was likewise confirmed in my opinion of your want of constancy and of the little importance you attached to the delicacy of the sentiment of love, when I witnessed what you did on board the Turkish vessel without being hindered by my presence; had you loved me, I thought my being present would have made you uncomfortable. I feared to be soon despised, and God knows how much I suffered! You have insulted me, darling, in many different ways, but my heart pleaded in your favour, because I knew you were excited, angry, and thirsting for revenge. Did you not threaten me this very day in your carriage? I confess you greatly frightened me, but do not fancy that I gave myself to you out of fear. No, I had made up my mind to be yours from the moment you sent me word by Cecilia that you would take me to Rimini, and your control over your own feelings during a part of our journey confirmed me in my resolution, for I thought I could trust myself to your honour, to your delicacy."

"Throw up," I said, "the engagement you have in Rimini; let us proceed on our journey, and, after remaining a couple of days in Bologna, you will go with me to Venice; dressed as a woman, and with another name, I would challenge the manager here to find you out."

"I accept. Your will shall always be my law. I am my own mistress, and I give myself to you without any reserve or restriction; my heart belongs to you, and I trust to keep yours."

Man has in himself a moral force of action which always makes him overstep the line on which he is standing. I had obtained everything, I wanted more. "Shew me," I said, "how you were when I mistook you for a man." She got out of bed, opened her trunk, took out the instrument and fixed it with the gum: I was compelled to admire the ingenuity of the contrivance. My curiosity was satisfied, and I passed a most delightful night in her arms.

When I woke up in the morning, I admired her lovely face while she was sleeping: all I knew of her came back to my mind; the words which had been spoken by her bewitching mouth, her rare talent, her candour, her feelings so full of delicacy, and her misfortunes, the heaviest of which must have been the false character she had been compelled to assume, and which exposed her to humiliation and shame, everything strengthened my resolution to make her the companion of my destiny, whatever it might be, or to follow her fate, for our positions were very nearly the same; and wishing truly to attach myself seriously to that interesting being, I determined to give to our union the sanction of religion and of law, and to take her legally for my wife. Such a step, as I then thought, could but strengthen our love, increase our mutual esteem, and insure the approbation of society which could not accept our union unless it was sanctioned in the usual manner.

The talents of Therese precluded the fear of our being ever in want of the necessaries of life, and, although I did not know in what way my own talents might be made available, I had faith in myself. Our love might have been lessened, she would have enjoyed too great advantages over me, and my self-dignity would have too deeply suffered if I had allowed myself to be supported by her earnings only. It might, after a time, have altered the nature of our feelings; my wife, no longer thinking herself under any obligation to me, might have fancied herself the protecting, instead of the protected party, and I felt that my love would soon have turned into utter contempt, if it had been my misfortune to find her harbouring such thoughts. Although I trusted it would not be so, I wanted, before taking the important step of marriage, to probe her heart, and I resolved to try an experiment which would at once enable me to judge the real feelings of her inmost soul. As soon as she was awake, I spoke to her thus:

"Dearest Therese, all you have told me leaves me no doubt of your love for me, and the consciousness you feel of being the mistress of my heart enhances my love for you to such a degree, that I am ready to do everything to convince you that you were not mistaken in thinking that you had entirely conquered me. I wish to prove to you that I am worthy of the noble confidence you have reposed in me by trusting you with equal sincerity.

"Our hearts must be on a footing of perfect equality. I know you, my dearest Therese, but you do not know me yet. I can read in your eyes that you do not mind it, and it proves our great love, but that feeling places me too much below you, and I do not wish you to have so great an advantage over me. I feel certain that my confidence is not necessary to your love; that you only care to be mine, that your only wish is to possess my heart, and I admire you, my Therese; but I should feel humiliated if I found myself either too much above or too much below you. You have entrusted your secrets to me, now listen to mine; but before I begin, promise me that, when you know everything that concerns me, you will tell me candidly if any change has taken place either in your feelings or in your hopes."

"I promise it faithfully; I promise not to conceal anything from you; but be upright enough not to tell me anything that is not perfectly true, for I warn you that it would be useless. If you tried any artifice in order to find me less worthy of you than I am in reality, you would only succeed in lowering yourself in my estimation. I should be very sorry to see you guilty of any cunning towards me. Have no more suspicion of me than I have of you; tell me the whole truth."

"Here it is. You suppose me wealthy, and I am not so; as soon as what there is now in my purse is spent I shall have nothing left. You may fancy that I was born a patrician, but my social condition is really inferior to your own. I have no lucrative talents, no profession, nothing to give me the assurance that I am able to earn my living. I have neither relatives nor friends, nor claims upon anyone, and I have no serious plan or purpose before me. All I possess is youth, health, courage, some intelligence, honour, honesty, and some tincture of letters. My greatest treasure consists in being my own master, perfectly independent, and not afraid of misfortune. With all that, I am naturally inclined to extravagance. Lovely Therese, you have my portrait. What is your answer?"

"In the first place, dearest, let me assure you that I believe every word you have just uttered, as I would believe in the Gospel; in the second, allow me to tell you that several times in Ancona I have judged you such as you have just described yourself, but far from being displeased at such a knowledge of your nature, I was only afraid of some illusion on my part, for I could hope to win you if you were what I thought you to be. In one word, dear one, if it is true that you are poor and a very bad hand at economy, allow me to tell you that I feel delighted, because, if you love me, you will not refuse a present from me, or despise me for offering it. The present consists of myself, such as I am, and with all my faculties. I give myself to you without any condition, with no restriction; I am yours, I will take care of you. For the future think only of your love for me, but love me exclusively. From this moment I am no longer Bellino. Let us go to Venice, where my talent will keep us both comfortably; if you wish to go anywhere else, let us go where you please."

"I must go to Constantinople."

"Then let us proceed to Constantinople. If you are afraid to lose me through want of constancy, marry me, and your right over me will be strengthened by law. I should not love you better than I do now, but I should be happy to be your wife."

"It is my intention to marry you, and I am delighted that we agree in that respect. The day after to-morrow, in Bologna, you shall be made my legal-wife before the altar of God; I swear it to you here in the presence of Love. I want you to be mine, I want to be yours, I want us to be united by the most holy ties."

"I am the happiest of women! We have nothing to do in Rimini; suppose we do not get up; we can have our dinner in bed, and go away to-morrow well rested after our fatigues."

We left Rimini the next day, and stayed for breakfast at Pesaro. As we were getting into the carriage to leave that place, an officer, accompanied by two soldiers, presented himself, enquired for our names, and demanded our passports. Bellino had one and gave it, but I looked in vain for mine; I could not find it.

The officer, a corporal, orders the postillion to wait and goes to make his report. Half an hour afterwards, he returns, gives Bellino his passport, saying that he can continue his journey, but tells me that his orders are to escort me to the commanding officer, and I follow him.

"What have you done with your passport?" enquires that officer.

"I have lost it."

"A passport is not so easily lost."

"Well, I have lost mine."

"You cannot proceed any further."

"I come from Rome, and I am going to Constantinople, bearing a letter from Cardinal Acquaviva. Here is the letter stamped with his seal."

"All I can do for you is to send you to M. de Gages."

I found the famous general standing, surrounded by his staff. I told him all I had already explained to the officer, and begged him to let me continue my journey.

"The only favour I can grant you is to put you under arrest till you receive another passport from Rome delivered under the same name as the one you have given here. To lose a passport is a misfortune which befalls only a thoughtless, giddy man, and the cardinal will for the future know better than to put his confidence in a giddy fellow like you."

With these words, he gave orders to take me to the guard-house at St. Mary's Gate, outside the city, as soon as I should have written to the cardinal for a new passport. His orders were executed. I was brought back to the inn, where I wrote my letter, and I sent it by express to his eminence, entreating him to forward the document, without loss of time, direct to the war office. Then I embraced Therese who was weeping, and, telling her to go to Rimini and to wait there for my return, I made her take one hundred sequins. She wished to remain in Pesaro, but I would not hear of it; I had my trunk brought out, I saw Therese go away from the inn, and was taken to the place appointed by the general.

It is undoubtedly under such circumstances that the most determined optimist finds himself at a loss; but an easy stoicism can blunt the too sharp edge of misfortune.

My greatest sorrow was the heart-grief of Therese who, seeing me torn from her arms at the very moment of our union, was suffocated by the tears which she tried to repress. She would not have left me if I had not made her understand that she could not remain in Pesaro, and if I had not promised to join her within ten days, never to be parted again. But fate had decided otherwise.

When we reached the gate, the officer confined me immediately in the guard-house, and I sat down on my trunk. The officer was a taciturn Spaniard who did not even condescend to honour me with an answer, when I told him that I had money and would like to have someone to wait on me. I had to pass the night on a little straw, and without food, in the midst of the Spanish soldiers. It was the second night of the sort that my destiny had condemned me to, immediately after two delightful nights. My good angel doubtless found some pleasure in bringing such conjunctions before my mind for the benefit of my instruction. At all events, teachings of that description have an infallible effect upon natures of a peculiar stamp.

If you should wish to close the lips of a logician calling himself a philosopher, who dares to argue that in this life grief overbalances pleasure, ask him whether he would accept a life entirely without sorrow and happiness. Be certain that he will not answer you, or he will shuffle, because, if he says no, he proves that he likes life such as it is, and if he likes it, he must find it agreeable, which is an utter impossibility, if life is painful; should he, on the contrary, answer in the affirmative, he would declare himself a fool, for it would be as much as to say that he can conceive pleasure arising from indifference, which is absurd nonsense.

Suffering is inherent in human nature; but we never suffer without entertaining the hope of recovery, or, at least, very seldom without such hope, and hope itself is a pleasure. If it happens sometimes that man suffers without any expectation of a cure, he necessarily finds pleasure in the complete certainty of the end of his life; for the worst, in all cases, must be either a sleep arising from extreme dejection, during which we have the consolation of happy dreams or the loss of all sensitiveness. But when we are happy, our happiness is never disturbed by the thought that it will be followed by grief. Therefore pleasure, during its active period, is always complete, without alloy; grief is always soothed by hope.

I suppose you, dear reader, at the age of twenty, and devoting yourself to the task of making a man of yourself by furnishing your mind with all the knowledge necessary to render you a useful being through the activity of your brain. Someone comes in and tells you, "I bring you thirty years of existence; it is the immutable decree of fate; fifteen consecutive years must be happy, and fifteen years unhappy. You are at liberty to choose the half by which you wish to begin."

Confess it candidly, dear reader, you will not require much more consideration to decide, and you will certainly begin by the unhappy series of years, because you will feel that the expectation of fifteen delightful years cannot fail to brace you up with the courage necessary to bear the unfortunate years you have to go through, and we can even surmise, with every probability of being right, that the certainty of future happiness will soothe to a considerable extent the misery of the first period.

You have already guessed, I have no doubt, the purpose of this lengthy argument. The sagacious man, believe me, can never be utterly miserable, and I most willingly agree with my friend Horace, who says that, on the contrary, such a man is always happy.

'Nisi quum pituita molesta est.'

But, pray where is the man who is always suffering from a rheum?

The fact is that the fearful night I passed in the guardhouse of St. Mary resulted for me in a slight loss and in a great gain. The small loss was to be away from my dear Therese, but, being certain of seeing her within ten days, the misfortune was not very great: as to the gain, it was in experience the true school for a man. I gained a complete system against thoughtlessness, a system of foresight. You may safely bet a hundred to one that a young man who has once lost his purse or his passport, will not lose either a second time. Each of those misfortunes has befallen me once only, and I might have been very often the victim of them, if experience had not taught me how much they were to be dreaded. A thoughtless fellow is a man who has not yet found the word dread in the dictionary of his life.

The officer who relieved my cross-grained Castilian on the following day seemed of a different nature altogether; his prepossessing countenance pleased me much. He was a Frenchman, and I must say that I have always liked the French, and never the Spaniards; there is in the manners of the first something so engaging, so obliging, that you feel attracted towards them as towards a friend, whilst an air of unbecoming haughtiness gives to the second a dark, forbidding countenance which certainly does not prepossess in their favour. Yet I have often been duped by Frenchmen, and never by Spaniards—a proof that we ought to mistrust our tastes.

The new officer, approaching me very politely, said to me,—

"To what chance, reverend sir, am I indebted for the honour of having you in my custody?"

Ah! here was a way of speaking which restored to my lungs all their elasticity! I gave him all the particulars of my misfortune, and he found the mishap very amusing. But a man disposed to laugh at my disappointment could not be disagreeable to me, for it proved that the turn of his mind had more than one point of resemblance with mine. He gave me at once a soldier to serve me, and I had very quickly a bed, a table, and a few chairs. He was kind enough to have my bed placed in his own room, and I felt very grateful to him for that delicate attention.

He gave me an invitation to share his dinner, and proposed a game of piquet afterwards, but from the very beginning he saw that I was no match for him; he told me so, and he warned me that the officer who would relieve him the next day was a better player even than he was himself; I lost three or four ducats. He advised me to abstain from playing on the following day, and I followed his advice. He told me also that he would have company to supper, that there would be a game of faro, but that the banker being a Greek and a crafty player, I ought not to play. I thought his advice very considerate, particularly when I saw that all the punters lost, and that the Greek, very calm in the midst of the insulting treatment of those he had duped, was pocketing his money, after handing a share to the officer who had taken an interest in the bank. The name of the banker was Don Pepe il Cadetto, and by his accent I knew he was a Neapolitan. I communicated my discovery to the officer, asking him why he had told me that the man was a Greek. He explained to me the meaning of the word greek applied to a gambler, and the lesson which followed his explanation proved very useful to me in after years.

During the five following days, my life was uniform and rather dull, but on the sixth day the same French officer was on guard, and I was very glad to see him. He told me, with a hearty laugh, that he was delighted to find me still in the guard-house, and I accepted the compliment for what it was worth. In the evening, we had the same bank at faro, with the same result as the first time, except a violent blow from the stick of one of the punters upon the back of the banker, of which the Greek stoically feigned to take no notice. I saw the same man again nine years afterwards in Vienna, captain in the service of Maria Theresa; he then called himself d'Afflisso. Ten years later, I found him a colonel, and some time after worth a million; but the last time I saw him, some thirteen or fourteen years ago, he was a galley slave. He was handsome, but (rather a singular thing) in spite of his beauty, he had a gallows look. I have seen others with the same stamp—Cagliostro, for instance, and another who has not yet been sent to the galleys, but who cannot fail to pay them a visit. Should the reader feel any curiosity about it, I can whisper the name in his ear.

Towards the ninth or tenth day everyone in the army knew and liked me, and I was expecting the passport, which could not be delayed much longer. I was almost free, and I would often walk about even out of sight of the sentinel. They were quite right not to fear my running away, and I should have been wrong if I had thought of escaping, but the most singular adventure of my life happened to me then, and most unexpectedly.

It was about six in the morning. I was taking a walk within one hundred yards of the sentinel, when an officer arrived and alighted from his horse, threw the bridle on the neck of his steed, and walked off. Admiring the docility of the horse, standing there like a faithful servant to whom his master has given orders to wait for him I got up to him, and without any purpose I get hold of the bridle, put my foot in the stirrup, and find myself in the saddle. I was on horseback for the first time in my life. I do not know whether I touched the horse with my cane or with my heels, but suddenly the animal starts at full speed. My right foot having slipped out of the stirrup, I press against the horse with my heels, and, feeling the pressure, it gallops faster and faster, for I did not know how to check it. At the last advanced post the sentinels call out to me to stop; but I cannot obey the order, and the horse carrying me away faster than ever, I hear the whizzing of a few musket balls, the natural consequence of my involuntary disobedience. At last, when I reach the first advanced picket of the Austrians, the horse is stopped, and I get off his back thanking God.

An officer of Hussars asks where I am running so fast, and my tongue, quicker than my thought, answers without any privity on my part, that I can render no account but to Prince Lobkowitz, commander-in-chief of the army, whose headquarters were at Rimini. Hearing my answer, the officer gave orders for two Hussars to get on horseback, a fresh one is given me, and I am taken at full gallop to Rimini, where the officer on guard has me escorted at once to the prince.

I find his highness alone, and I tell him candidly what has just happened to me. My story makes him laugh, although he observes that it is hardly credible.

"I ought," he says, "to put you under arrest, but I am willing to save you that unpleasantness." With that he called one of his officers and ordered him to escort me through the Cesena Gate. "Then you can go wherever you please," he added, turning round to me; "but take care not to again enter the lines of my army without a passport, or you might fare badly."

I asked him to let me have the horse again, but he answered that the animal did not belong to me. I forgot to ask him to send me back to the place I had come from, and I regretted it; but after all perhaps I did for the best.

The officer who accompanied me asked me, as we were passing a coffee-house, whether I would like to take some chocolate, and we went in. At that moment I saw Petronio going by, and availing myself of a moment when the officer was talking to someone, I told him not to appear to be acquainted with me, but to tell me where he lived. When we had taken our chocolate the officer paid and we went out. Along the road we kept up the conversation; he told me his name, I gave him mine, and I explained how I found myself in Rimini. He asked me whether I had not remained some time in Ancona; I answered in the affirmative, and he smiled and said I could get a passport in Bologna, return to Rimini and to Pesaro without any fear, and recover my trunk by paying the officer for the horse he had lost. We reached the gate, he wished me a pleasant journey, and we parted company.

I found myself free, with gold and jewels, but without my trunk. Therese was in Rimini, and I could not enter that city. I made up my mind to go to Bologna as quickly as possible in order to get a passport, and to return to Pesaro, where I should find my passport from Rome, for I could not make up my mind to lose my trunk, and I did not want to be separated from Therese until the end of her engagement with the manager of the Rimini Theatre.

It was raining; I had silk stockings on, and I longed for a carriage. I took shelter under the portal of a church, and turned my fine overcoat inside out, so as not to look like an abbe. At that moment a peasant happened to come along, and I asked him if a carriage could be had to drive me to Cesena. "I have one, sir," he said, "but I live half a league from here."

"Go and get it, I will wait for you here."

While I was waiting for the return of the peasant with his vehicle, some forty mules laden with provisions came along the road towards Rimini. It was still raining fast, and the mules passing close by me, I placed my hand mechanically upon the neck of one of them, and following the slow pace of the animals I re-entered Rimini without the slightest notice being taken of me, even by the drivers of the mules. I gave some money to the first street urchin I met, and he took me to Therese's house.

With my hair fastened under a night-cap, my hat pulled down over my face, and my fine cane concealed under my coat, I did not look a very elegant figure. I enquired for Bellino's mother, and the mistress of the house took me to a room where I found all the family, and Therese in a woman's dress. I had reckoned upon surmising them, but Petronio had told them of our meeting, and they were expecting me. I gave a full account of my adventures, but Therese, frightened at the danger that threatened me, and in spite of her love, told me that it was absolutely necessary for me to go to Bologna, as I had been advised by M. Vais, the officer.

"I know him," she said, "and he is a worthy man, but he comes here every evening, and you must conceal yourself."

It was only eight o'clock in the morning; we had the whole day before us, and everyone promised to be discreet. I allayed Therese's anxiety by telling her that I could easily contrive to leave the city without being observed.

Therese took me to her own room, where she told me that she had met the manager of the theatre on her arrival in Rimini, and that he had taken her at once to the apartments engaged for the family. She had informed him that she was a woman, and that she had made up her mind not to appear as a castrato any more; he had expressed himself delighted at such news, because women could appear on the stage at Rimini, which was not under the same legate as Ancona. She added that her engagement would be at an end by the 1st of May, and that she would meet me wherever it would be agreeable to me to wait for her.

"As soon as I can get a passport," I said, "there is nothing to hinder me from remaining near you until the end of your engagement. But as M. Vais calls upon you, tell me whether you have informed him of my having spent a few days in Ancona?"

"I did, and I even told him that you had been arrested because you had lost your passport."

I understood why the officer had smiled as he was talking with me. After my conversation with Therese, I received the compliments of the mother and of the young sisters who appeared to me less cheerful and less free than they had been in Ancona. They felt that Bellino, transformed into Therese, was too formidable a rival. I listened patiently to all the complaints of the mother who maintained that, in giving up the character of castrato, Therese had bidden adieu to fortune, because she might have earned a thousand sequins a year in Rome.

"In Rome, my good woman," I said, "the false Bellino would have been found out, and Therese would have been consigned to a miserable convent for which she was never made."

Notwithstanding the danger of my position, I spent the whole of the day alone with my beloved mistress, and it seemed that every moment gave her fresh beauties and increased my love. At eight o'clock in the evening, hearing someone coming in, she left me, and I remained in the dark, but in such a position that I could see everything and hear every word. The Baron Vais came in, and Therese gave him her hand with the grace of a pretty woman and the dignity of a princess. The first thing he told her was the news about me; she appeared to be pleased, and listened with well-feigned indifference, when he said that he had advised me to return with a passport. He spent an hour with her, and I was thoroughly well pleased with her manners and behaviour, which had been such as to leave me no room for the slightest feeling of jealousy. Marina lighted him out and Therese returned to me. We had a joyous supper together, and, as we were getting ready to go to bed, Petronio came to inform me that ten muleteers would start for Cesena two hours before day-break, and that he was sure I could leave the city with them if I would go and meet them a quarter of an hour before their departure, and treat them to something to drink. I was of the same opinion, and made up my mind to make the attempt. I asked Petronio to sit up and to wake me in good time. It proved an unnecessary precaution, for I was ready before the time, and left Therese satisfied with my love, without any doubt of my constancy, but rather anxious as to my success in attempting to leave Rimini. She had sixty sequins which she wanted to force back upon me, but I asked her what opinion she would have of me if I accepted them, and we said no more about it.

I went to the stable, and having treated one of the muleteers to some drink I told him that I would willingly ride one of his mules as far as Sarignan.

"You are welcome to the ride," said the good fellow, "but I would advise you not to get on the mule till we are outside the city, and to pass through the gate on foot as if you were one of the drivers."

It was exactly what I wanted. Petronio accompanied me as far as the gate, where I gave him a substantial proof of my gratitude. I got out of the city without the slightest difficulty, and left the muleteers at Sarignan, whence I posted to Bologna.

I found out that I could not obtain a passport, for the simple reason that the authorities of the city persisted that it was not necessary; but I knew better, and it was not for me to tell them why. I resolved to write to the French officer who had treated me so well at the guardhouse. I begged him to enquire at the war office whether my passport had arrived from Rome, and, if so, to forward it to me. I also asked him to find out the owner of the horse who had run away with me, offering to pay for it. I made up my mind to wait for Therese in Bologna, and I informed her of my decision, entreating her to write very often. The reader will soon know the new resolution I took on the very same day.

A Note About the Author

Giacomo Casanova (1725–1798) was an Italian adventurer and author. Born in Venice, Casanova was the eldest of six siblings born to Gaetano Casanova and Zanetta Farussi, an actor and actress. Raised in a city noted for its cosmopolitanism, night life, and glamor, Casanova overcame a sickly childhood to excel in school, entering the University of Padua at the age of 12. After graduating in 1742 with a degree in law, he struggled to balance his work as a lawyer and low-level cleric with a growing gambling addiction. As scandals and a prison sentence threatened to derail his career in the church, Casanova managed to find work as a scribe for a powerful Cardinal in Rome, but was soon dismissed and entered military service for the Republic of Venice. Over the next several years, he left the service, succeeded as a professional gambler, and embarked on a Grand Tour of Europe. Towards the end of his life, Casanova worked on his exhaustive, scandalous memoirs, a 12-volume autobiography reflecting on a legendary life of romance and debauchery that brought him from the heights of aristocratic society to the lows of illness and imprisonment. Recognized for his self-styled sensationalism as much as he is for his detailed chronicling of 18th century European culture, Casanova is a man whose name is now synonymous with the kind of life he led—fast, fearless, and free.

A Note from the Publisher

Spanning many genres, from non-fiction essays to literature classics to children's books and lyric poetry, Mint Edition books showcase the master works of our time in a modern new package. The text is freshly typeset, is clean and easy to read, and features a new note about the author in each volume. Many books also include exclusive new introductory material. Every book boasts a striking new cover, which makes it as appropriate for collecting as it is for gift giving. Mint Edition books are only printed when a reader orders them, so natural resources are not wasted. We're proud that our books are never manufactured in excess and exist only in the exact quantity they need to be read and enjoyed.

bookfinity™

Discover more of your favorite classics with Bookfinity™.

- Track your reading with custom book lists.
- Get great book recommendations for your personalized Reader Type.
- Add reviews for your favorite books.
- AND MUCH MORE!

Visit **bookfinity.com** and take the fun Reader Type quiz to get started.

Enjoy our classic and modern companion pairings!